Childhood-Onset Eating Problems: Findings from Research

BY CLAUDINE FOX & CAROL JOUGHIN

Gaskell is an imprint of the Royal College of Psychiatrists, 17 Belgrave Square, London SW1X 8PG.

British Library Cataloguing-in-Publication Data
A catalogue record for this book is available from the British Library.
ISBN 1-901242-76-5

The views presented in this book do not necessarily reflect those of the Royal College of Psychiatrists, and the publishers are not responsible for any error of omission or fact.

Gaskell is a registered trademark of the Royal College of Psychiatrists.
The Royal College of Psychiatrists is a registered charity (no. 228636).

Printed by Cromwell Press Ltd, Trowbridge, UK.

Cover artwork © Catherine Brighton, 2001

contents

acknowledgements

The FOCUS Project is funded by a grant from the Gatsby Charitable Foundation and the Department of Health (Section 64 Grant Award).

We are grateful to the following experts who provided us with advice and comments on early drafts of this report:

Rachel Bryant-Waugh
Consultant Clinical Psychologist, Department of Psychological Medicine, Great Ormond Street Hospital for Children, Great Ormond Street, London WC1N 3JH

Jo Douglas
Consultant Clinical Psychologist, Ladymead, Loudwater Heights, Rickmansworth, Hertfordshire WD3 4AX. Formerly Consultant Clinical Psychologist, Department of Psychological Medicine, Great Ormond Street Hospital for Children, Great Ormond Street, London WC1N 3JH

Bryan Lask
Consultant Psychiatrist, Department of Psychiatry, Jenner Wing, St George's Hospital Medical School, Cranmer Terrace, London SW17 0RE; and South West London & St George's Mental Health NHS Trust and Huntercombe Manor Hospital, Taplow, Berkshire SL6 0PQ

Dasha Nicholls
Clinical Lecturer, Institute of Child Health, 30 Guilford Street, London, WC1N 1EH; and Research Fellow, Department of Psychological Medicine, Great Ormond Street Hospital for Children, Great Ormond Street, London WC1N 3JH

preface

In recent years, eating problems in childhood and adolescence have become a major public health issue. Problems at this stage in the life course have a huge potential impact on the growth and development of the child and cause high anxiety for parents and carers.

It is only relatively recently that children with eating problems have come to be regarded as a subgroup. Literature on all aspects of eating problems that specifically relates to children is limited, little is known about the nature, type and long-term outlook of the different disorders found and there is confusion in terms of classification.

This report therefore aims to provide a resource collating current information on eating problems in children in order to highlight the current understanding and position of research within the field. The report is primarily concerned with children between the ages of 5 and 12 years; however, there is no definitive age at which children can suffer from the eating problems described. It does not include issues relating to failure to thrive in infancy, and although eating problems in pre-school children, anorexia nervosa and bulimia are discussed, they are not the focus of this report.

The report identifies the different types of problems that are found, provides information on how prevalent eating problems are within this age group, highlights research that has identified risk factors for developing eating difficulties and why they arise and provides information on what can be done to treat the different disorders and what the long-term outlook is. Following this, Chapter 7 focuses on research that has been conducted within the field; it provides an overview and includes critical appraisal of key research papers. Finally, we have included a glossary of terms and a list of useful addresses.

It is hoped that this report will provide a central source of information that will provide answers to common questions about childhood-onset eating problems.

introduction

The majority of pre-school children will, at some time in the first five years of life, experience some problems with eating. For example, they may only eat a small number of different foods, eat very little or refuse to eat altogether. For most of these children, this is a passing phase and they will grow out of it. However, for some the eating problem is more severe and may be longer lasting. The aim of this report is to provide professionals with information regarding childhood-onset eating problems. It is primarily concerned with children between the ages of 5 and 12 years; however, there is no definitive age at which children can suffer from the eating problems described. The report does not include issues relating to failure to thrive in infancy, and although eating problems in pre-school children, anorexia nervosa and bulimia are discussed, they are not the focus of this report.

It is only within the past two decades that children with eating problems have come to be regarded as a subgroup of interest. Literature on all aspects of eating problems that specifically relates to children is sparse. The majority of what is known about childhood-onset eating problems has therefore been obtained through clinical experience and expertise and not through evidence based on robust research.

The eating problems that are found in childhood differ in terms of aetiology, clinical presentation and treatment from those found in late adolescence or in adult life. A greater number of varying types of eating problems are found in this younger age group. Furthermore, there are greater long-term physical and psychological implications for a child experiencing eating problems compared with an adult suffering from an eating disorder.

The nature of the various disorders found in childhood has caused debate and confusion, leaving the position regarding childhood-onset eating problems unclear (Lask & Bryant-Waugh, 2000). This has arisen for a number of reasons.

First, there is confusion in the literature regarding the terminology used to describe eating problems in children, where a variety of terms may be used. The names of the types of disorders found are purely descriptive and have been created by those working in the field, out of a need for a language to talk about the children that present to them for treatment. Variation in the language used has arisen owing to the large number of different professions that may be involved in the treatment of children with eating problems, for example psychology, psychiatry, speech therapy, physiotherapy, nutrition and dietetics, to name but a few. More specifically, and to add to the confusion, when reading the literature the word 'problem' may be used interchangeably with 'disorder'; however, 'disorder' in some cases is used to indicate a greater degree of severity. 'Feeding' is often used when talking about problems occurring in infancy or early childhood, owing to the interactive nature of eating during this period, and the term 'eating disorder' is commonly used to refer to eating problems found in adolescence and adulthood.

Second, confusion has arisen owing to the continuum of eating and feeding difficulties, in that in pre-school children feeding difficulties are relatively common and seen as developmentally normal. At this age, children are experimenting with new tastes and textures and also the impact that their behaviour has on their carer. In these cases, the eating problem is correctly described as 'a phase' that the child will grow out of as he or she matures. However, eating problems in older children should be seen in a very different light; for example, an eight-year-old child presenting with selective eating (extreme faddiness). Here, the eating problem is not appropriate to the child's stage of development, as older children have developed a more sophisticated cognitive ability. This means that the eating problem may be related to underlying psychological issues.

Finally, to add to the confusion, there is a lack of standardised instruments for the assessment of eating disorders in childhood. This has meant that much of the published research has been based on methodology utilising a clinical case report design (Lask & Bryant-Waugh, 2000).

Lask & Bryant-Waugh (2000) point out that two common myths regarding eating disorders in children have emerged. The first postulates that we are currently seeing an 'epidemic' of childhood-onset eating disorders. Eating problems in children are relatively rare and the general increase in weight sensitivity observed within the childhood population does not necessarily play a causal role in the development of eating disorders. The second myth states that eating problems in the childhood population are a new phenomenon; however, childhood-onset eating problems were described as early as 1894 (Collins) and 1895 (Marshall).

Before proceeding, a few points need to be taken into account. Childhood-onset eating problems within the context of this report refer to children between the ages of 5 and 12 years. It is also important to point out that, owing to the confusion in terminology, the term 'eating problems' will be used to describe the problematic eating behaviours exhibited by these children. In addition, when referring to a disorder, if alternative names are relevant these will be presented in brackets following each term, for example where 'restrictive eating' is referred to, 'poor appetite' will follow in brackets. It is hoped that this will help to clarify the terminology used.

one types of eating problem

The eating problems that children suffer from are very different to those experienced by adolescents and adults. There are a larger number of different eating problems found in children, which have different causes, different characteristics and need different forms of treatment. Also, some of the eating problems found, for example childhood-onset anorexia nervosa and food avoidance emotional disorder, have a more serious effect on the child's physical and psychological well-being compared with others, for example restrictive eating (poor appetite) and selective eating (extreme faddiness).

CLASSIFICATION

A classification of mental disorders is important for clinical practice, research and statistical information. At the present time, there are two widely recognised classification systems. These are the DSM–IV (American Psychiatric Association (APA), 1994) and the ICD–10 (World Health Organization (WHO), 1992). These systems provide criteria for the identification of the different mental disorders, enabling diagnosis and treatment, identification and comparison of different groups of individuals.

As mentioned already, the names of the eating problems found in childhood are purely descriptive and have been created by those working in the field in order to describe the children that present to them for treatment. This is a consequence of there being no standardised classification system for the eating problems found in school-age children. In fact, neither the ICD–10 nor the DSM–IV offers diagnostic categories appropriate for the diagnosis of childhood-onset eating problems.

As a result, alternative methods of classification of have arisen. These have been descriptive (Lask & Bryant-Waugh, 1993; APA, 1994; Babbitt *et al*, 1994a), causal (Budd *et al*, 1992; Linscheid, 1992) and multidimensional (Chatoor *et al*, 1985) approaches. Lask & Bryant-Waugh (2000) have suggested a useful method using working definitions of the different types of eating problems found in children (see Box 1.1).

Research has given support to the existence of the different types of disorder put forward by Lask & Bryant-Waugh (2000). Cooper *et al* at the Academy of Eating Disorders 9th International Conference in New York (2000) presented a study that aimed to clarify the psychopathology of childhood-onset eating problems. The study consisted of 126 patients who had been referred to a specialist eating disorder service. Eighty-eight presented with an early-onset eating disorder (girls who were pre-menarchal and boys who were pre-pubertal at onset) and the remaining 34 later-onset. Among the early-onset group, 43% had a diagnosis of anorexia nervosa, 29% a diagnosis of food avoidance emotional disorder (FAED), 19% selective eating and 9% another eating disorder such as functional dysphagia. Results indicated that children in the early-onset anorexia nervosa group showed a similar level of disturbance to that present in the later-onset group. The authors concluded that the study confirmed the diagnostic validity of early-onset anorexia nervosa.

EATING PROBLEMS

The following sections provide a brief description of each of the eating problems found in children. It is also important to point out that the descriptions given are true for the majority of children who present with each condition. For example, children who present with selective eating (extreme faddiness), restrictive eating (poor appetite), food refusal and inappropriate texture of food for age will usually have no problems with health or growth. However, a very small number of children presenting with these conditions will have a problem with health and/or growth. This is particularly true if the problem has continued for a number of years.

Childhood-onset anorexia nervosa

Children with anorexia nervosa are preoccupied with their weight and body shape. They have a distorted view of their body and an abnormal or inadequate intake of food. They have a strong need to lose weight and so avoid eating in order to do so. If they have to eat, then they will eat as little as they possibly can in terms of quantity or they will avoid foods that contain a large amount of calories. These children still feel hungry, and sometimes the feelings of hunger may be so strong that they have to eat. Having done so, they will feel very guilty and have to get rid of what they have just eaten. This may be in the form of making themselves sick, taking laxatives or exercising. In terms of personality characteristics, people that develop anorexia nervosa tend to have perfectionist tendencies and will set themselves high standards, which they will then work hard to achieve.

Childhood-onset bulimia nervosa

Children with bulimia nervosa frequently engage in binges, in that they will eat excessive quantities of food at one time. A binge may consist of eating up to four times the amount that would constitute a normal meal for most people. They may eat unusual combinations of food or eat large amounts of the same food. Having binged, these children will feel very guilty for having done so. They will therefore make themselves sick in order to get rid of the food that they have just ingested. Alternatively, they may use laxatives in an attempt to control weight gain. Children with bulimia nervosa are also preoccupied with their weight and body shape. They make judgements about themselves on the basis of the way that they think that they look. They are extremely critical of themselves and think that they are worthless. Their weight may be low, normal or high, so it can be more difficult to ascertain that a child is suffering from bulimia nervosa.

Pervasive refusal syndrome

This is a very serious condition where children present with a profound refusal to walk, talk, eat, drink or care for themselves in any way. Physical examination provides no organic explanation for the symptoms. These children are often very determined, angry or frightened. Their families deny any conflicts or other problems; however, there are often histories of violence within the family. It also appears that a history of sexual abuse contributes to this problem.

Box 1.1 Working definitions of the different types of eating problems found in children (adapted with permission from Lask & Bryant-Waugh, 2000)

Childhood-onset anorexia nervosa
(i)   Determined weight loss
(ii)   Abnormal cognitions regarding weight and/or shape
(iii) Morbid preoccupation with weight and/or shape, food and/or eating

Childhood-onset bulimia nervosa
(i)   Recurrent binges and purges and/or food restriction
(ii)   Sense of lack of control
(iii) Abnormal cognitions regarding weight and/or shape

Food avoidance emotional disorder (FAED)
(i)   Food avoidance
(ii)   Weight loss
(iii) Mood disturbance
(iv)   No abnormal cognitions regarding weight and/or shape
(v)   No morbid preoccupation with weight and/or shape
(vi)   No organic brain disease, psychosis, illicit drug use, or prescribed drug-related side-effects

Selective eating/extreme faddiness
(i)   Narrow range of foods (for at least two years)
(ii)   Unwillingness to try new foods
(iii) No abnormal cognitions regarding weight and/or shape
(iv)   No morbid preoccupation with weight and/or shape
(v)   Weight may be low, normal or high

Restrictive eating/poor appetite
(i)   Smaller than usual amounts for age eaten
(ii)   Diet normal in terms of nutritional content but not in amount
(iii) No abnormal cognitions regarding weight and/or shape
(iv)   No morbid preoccupation with weight and/or shape
(v)   Weight and height tend to be low

Food refusal
(i)   Food refusal tends to be episodic, intermittent or situational
(ii)   No abnormal cognitions regarding weight and/or shape
(iii) No morbid preoccupation with weight and/or shape

Functional dysphagia/food phobia
(i)   Food avoidance
(ii)   Fear of swallowing, choking or vomiting
(iii) No abnormal cognitions regarding weight and/or shape
(iv)   No morbid preoccupation with weight and/or shape

Pervasive refusal syndrome
(i)   Profound refusal to eat, drink, walk, talk, or self-care
(ii)   Determined resistance to efforts to help

Food avoidance emotional disorder

Children who suffer from FAED are usually between the ages of five and 16 years. The presenting symptoms of this condition may be confused with that of anorexia nervosa or an emotional disorder, such as depression or anxiety. These children have difficulties with eating but cannot be diagnosed with any of the other types of eating problems. The concept of this disorder is that the children experience some emotional problems, for example sadness, worries or obsessionality, which interfere with their appetite and eating. These children are not preoccupied with their weight or body shape and in fact may even express that they recognise that they need to put on weight, but do not feel hungry.

Functional dysphagia/food phobia

In general, these children are fearful of eating, and in particular of eating lumpy or solid foods. They do not want to put food into their mouths and swallow it for fear that it may poison them, or cause them to gag, choke or vomit. These children are not preoccupied with their body shape and do not want to lose weight. They may have experienced some traumatic incident that has triggered the phobia. Alternatively, they may have made a peculiar or illogical association in their mind that may lead to them developing the phobia.

Selective eating/extreme faddiness

It is believed that children who suffer from selective eating or extreme faddiness have not grown out of the normal developmental phase of eating a restricted range of foods. This is commonly seen in pre-school children. These children eat a very narrow range of foods – maybe just five or six that are usually carbohydrate-based – and do not like to try new foods. It is hard to get them to try new foods and when presented with a novel food type, they may wretch. These children have no difficulty in swallowing or keeping down their favoured foods, however. Children with selective eating (extreme faddiness) tend to be of normal weight and height and are healthy. They seem to acquire adequate calories to sustain growth and development. In terms of cause, there is sometimes a history of a close relative having had a similar problem, but there is no underlying organic cause to explain the symptoms. These children are not preoccupied with their weight or body shape, and are usually seen between the ages of seven and 11 years. This is because at this age they start to go to school and socialise more with other children, so they can no longer get away with 'faddy' eating as they did when they were younger.

Restrictive eating/poor appetite

Children who suffer from restrictive eating or poor appetite seem not to eat very much at all. They will eat a normal range of foods, but have a small appetite and seem disinterested in food. These children are not preoccupied with their weight, do not want to lose weight and seem perfectly happy. This condition is more common in the pre-school years and is relatively harmless as children tend to grow and develop in the normal way. If the problem persists for several years, however, it may have an impact on the growth of the child and so may become problematic. It is important to ascertain that the restrictive eating (poor appetite) is not owing to associated emotional problems.

Food refusal

This is commonly found in pre-school children, where the food refusal can be used as a means to obtain other things. However, this can persist in slightly older children and is characterised by an inconsistent avoidance of food. They tend to eat favourite foods without any problem at all. They may only refuse food when in the presence of particular people or in certain situations, for example refusing to eat at school but eating normally at home. These children are not preoccupied with weight and shape, and tend not to have any weight problems. Worry or unhappiness may underlie the food refusal in many cases. This problem does not usually pose a threat to the child's health and well-being.

Inappropriate texture of food for age

These children eat only pureed or semi-solid food, which is appropriate for a 6–10-month-old infant, when they should be eating a normal solid diet of food that requires biting and chewing. If presented with lumps in their food they may spit the food out, gag or refuse to eat it altogether. In addition, these children may or may not refuse to eat finger foods. The majority of children will have their weight well-maintained on the inappropriate textures; however, some will be of low weight. Although children eat a full range of food types, parents tend to show concern about the impact that this disorder has on the social functioning of the child. For example, in children over four years of age, this causes great concern where difficulties arise around school lunchtimes.

IDENTIFICATION OF CHILDHOOD-ONSET EATING PROBLEMS

Before referral to child and adolescent mental health services (CAMHS), families with children with eating problems may spend a number of months seeking advice from various health professionals. In fact, one study has found an average of 7.4 months between initially requesting professional

Table 1.1 Summary of the types of eating problems

Eating problem	Pre-school	School age	Adolescence
Childhood-onset anorexia nervosa	✕	✓	✓✓
Childhood-onset bulimia nervosa	✕	✓	✓✓
Pervasive refusal syndrome (syndrome rare)	✕	✓✓	✓
Food avoidance emotional disorder	✕	✓✓	✓
Functional dysphagia/food phobia (syndrome rare)	✕	✓✓	✓
Selective eating/extreme faddiness (quality)	✓✓	✓✓	✓
Restrictive eating/poor appetite (quantity)	✓✓	✓✓	✓
Food refusal	✓✓	✓	✕
Inappropriate texture of food for age (texture)	✓✓	✓	✕

✓✓ , disorder mostly found in this age group; ✓ , disorder sometimes found in this age group; ✕, disorder does not occur in this age group

help and referral to specialist services (Fosson *et al*, 1987). This delay in referral has been linked to doctors not recognising the eating problems that children suffer from. Some empirical research investigating older patients with eating disorders has found that a shorter history of illness is a predictor of good outcome (Morgan & Russell, 1975; Hsu *et al*, 1979). This raises questions in terms of the treatment of eating problems in children, as a longer referral period may lead to the eating problem becoming more established and difficult to treat.

Bryant-Waugh *et al* (1992) carried out a study in order to investigate whether doctors recognise eating problems in children. Paediatricians, school doctors and general practitioners were presented with two short vignettes describing common presenting features of childhood-onset anorexia nervosa. They were then asked questions regarding diagnosis and management. The authors found that the awareness of childhood-onset eating problems was limited. This was particularly true in the case of doctors.

Simple diagnostic flowchart

In utilising the working definitions proposed by Lask & Bryant-Waugh (2000), it has been possible to construct a diagnostic flowchart. The chart incorporates a number of important features that may be used to identify the eating problems found in children. This is achieved through answering the questions presented in the flowchart (see Fig. 1.1).

It is important to note, however, that this is a simple diagnostic flowchart – alternative diagnoses that are not included in the chart should not therefore be ruled out. For example, if a child presents with low weight and short stature, then the following diagnoses are all possibilities: genetic syndromes, such as silver Russel syndrome and Turner syndrome, gastrointestinal disease, endocrine disease or renal disease. These conditions, although rare (they occur in less than 5% of short children), are all possibilities.

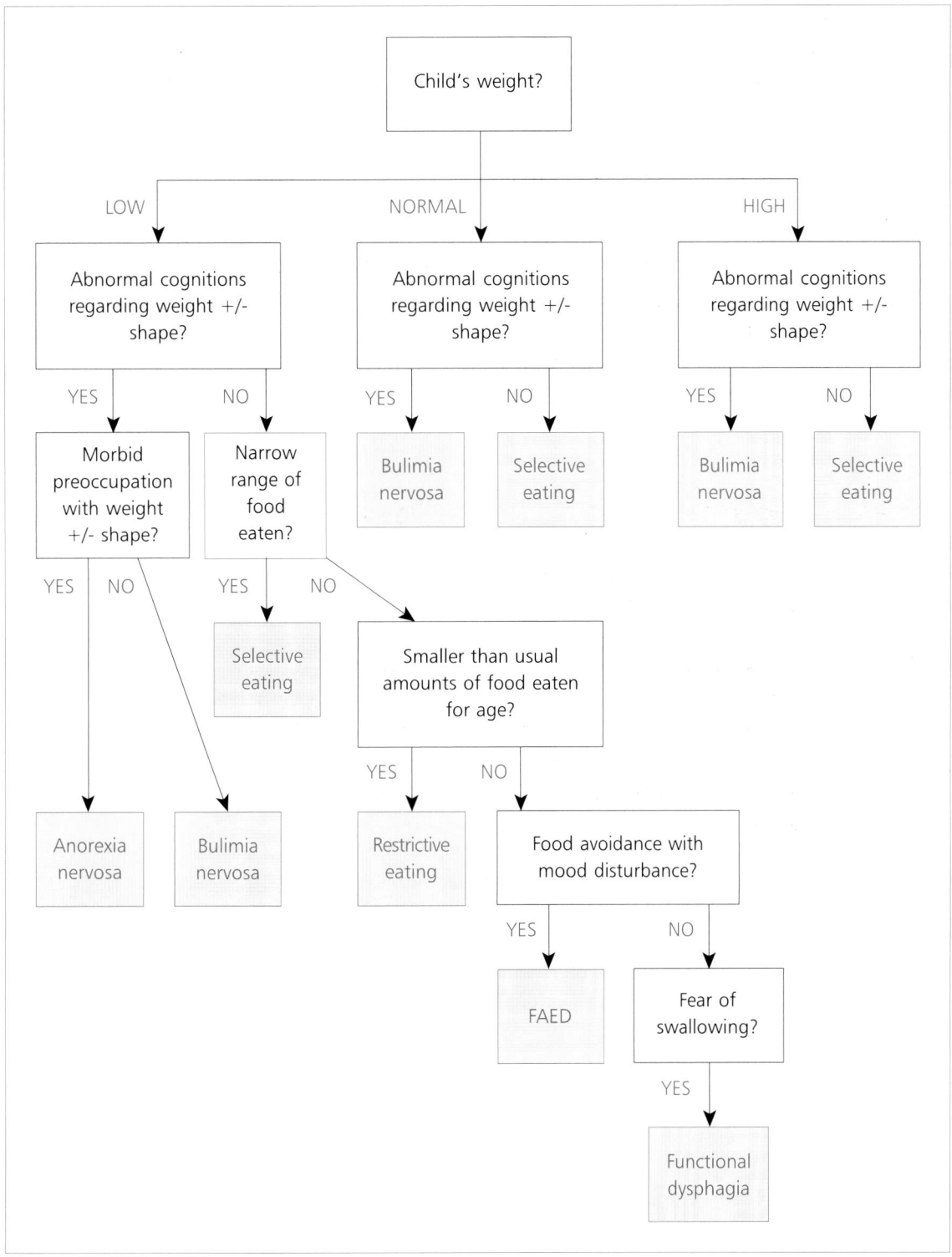

Fig. 1.1 A simple diagnostic flowchart for the eating problems found in childhood

incidence and prevalence

Incidence figures provide information on the frequency of occurrence of a condition in relation to a population. Prevalence is slightly different in that it is the total number of cases of a disease or a disorder in a population at a specific point in time. In order to establish precise figures, large-scale studies need to be conducted. The lack of consistent diagnostic criteria within the field of childhood-onset eating problems has led to an absence of large-scale studies, meaning that precise incidence and prevalence figures are not available. However, the studies that have been carried out have provided a limited amount of information. These can be divided into those that investigate the general population and those that look at clinical populations.

GENERAL POPULATION

Studies investigating the prevalence rates of eating problems in normal British children have found that one-third of children by the age of five years have had mild to moderate eating difficulties. Of this group, two-thirds suffer from faddy eating and the rest do not eat enough. Eating problems were also found to be more prevalent in low-birth-weight babies but less prevalent in large families (Butler & Golding, 1986).

Another prevalence study conducted in London found that 16% of three-year-olds suffer with poor appetite and 12% of three-year-olds are faddy eaters (Richman et al, 1982).

Estimates of the duration of these problems range from one year in about two-thirds of children to five years in about one-third. Of the under-one-year-olds, 71% continue to have a problem until the age of four years (Dahl & Sundelin, 1992).

CLINICAL POPULATION

It has been estimated that one-third of children with developmental delay suffer from meal-time problems, a figure that rises to 80% where the children suffer with severe learning disabilities (Perske et al, 1977).

Children with severe physical disabilities are also at risk for eating problems, for example children who suffer from cerebral palsy. In this case, the eating difficulty has an organic basis owing to a disorganised swallowing mechanism (Douglas, 1995a).

Research has shown that children with chronic illness are at greater risk for developing eating problems (Culbert et al, 1996). Baer (1997) states that between 10% and 42% of children with chronic illnesses suffer from eating problems. Illnesses include kidney conditions, liver disease, cystic fibrosis, cancer and diabetes.

Douglas & Bryon (1996) looked at children who had been referred to the pre-school eating problems programme at the Department of Psychological Medicine at Great Ormond Street Hospital. They found that 78% of the children suffered from inadequate quantity of food eaten (restrictive eating or poor appetite), 34% from severe selective eating (extreme faddiness) and 50% from inappropriate texture of food for age.

As the scale of the problem is unclear owing to a lack of good epidemiological research with this population, an alternative source of information on incidence and prevalence is to look at the demand for services. There are fewer patients with eating disorders aged between 8 and 13 years than there are aged between 14 and 19 years. Resources for younger patients are limited, which may reflect that demands have not been high. Over the past decade, a significant increase in the number of referrals to the school-age clinic at the Department of Psychological Medicine, Great Ormond Street Hospital has been noticed. However, it is important to note that although this may well reflect a rise in the number of children developing eating disorders, it may also reflect an increase in awareness that these eating disorders can occur in children or even an increase in the knowledge that specialist services are available (Lask & Bryant-Waugh, 2000).

three aetiology and maintaining factors

The exact aetiology and factors that maintain eating problems in children are still relatively unknown – again this is owing to the lack of research that has been conducted within this area. However, eating problems in children are not due to a single causative factor, but result from a large number of interacting factors. These may be psychological, biological or sociocultural. Eating problems develop over time, with some causal factors being in place from birth, while other factors will develop at various times during the life span (Lask & Bryant-Waugh, 2000).

Aetiology and maintaining factors may be looked at in terms of predisposing, precipitating and perpetuating factors. Predisposing factors need to be present for the development of the eating problem. For example, the child may have a genetic vulnerability, a certain type of personality or particular sociocultural demands. Precipitating factors serve to trigger the condition. These may be stressors such as pubertal development, low self-esteem, family problems, or school and peer-group problems. Finally, perpetuating factors maintain the eating problem once it has started. These include types of management of the problem and the sense of achievement felt by the child in gaining control over the body and the effects of starvation. The picture becomes complicated when predisposing factors such as sociocultural demands precipitate the problem; in addition, any of the precipitating factors mentioned may perpetuate the problem.

In pre-school children, two different types of maintaining factors have been identified. These are grouped as 'organic' and 'non-organic' factors. Organic factors include physical abnormalities, for example mechanical obstruction or cranial nerve damage. Non-organic factors include environmental factors that have consequences on feeding behaviour, for example, a lack of exposure to developmentally appropriate food texture, inadequate parental supervision and behavioural mismanagement (Babbitt et al, 1994a).

Many children with eating problems have had a past history of organic (physical) difficulties, which influenced their early feeding experience as babies. Subsequently, even when the organic problems have been resolved, the child is often left with a psychologically based eating problem (Douglas & Bryon, 1996).

Parent–child interactions also influence the development of the feeding process. Certain interaction types can cause feeding problems – for example, a child may gain attention through behaviours such as crying, throwing food, spitting and pushing food away. Alternatively, refusing to eat, eating only a narrow range of foods or eating very little may be the only way the child feels that he or she can exert control over his or her world and may use these behaviours to express how he or she is feeling, for example distressed or sad. This in turn causes an increase in parental anxiety, so affecting the parent–child relationship around feeding times (Babbitt *et al*, 1994a).

Children who are slow feeders early on show poor appetites (restrictive eating) or may seem disinterested in food later in childhood. Pressure from health care professionals for the mother to feed the child can increase parental anxiety to such an extent that it produces tense and unpleasant meal-times (Douglas & Bryon, 1996).

Early adverse feeding experiences such as vomiting repeatedly and unpleasant internal sensations associated with eating, for example gastro-oesophageal reflux, choking and gagging with solids, produce a conditioned response of food avoidance seen in children who refuse solids (food refusal) (Douglas & Bryon, 1996).

A disordered early feeding experience, for example long periods of naso-gastric feeding, neuro-logical difficulties or immature oral–motor skills may affect the child's experience of normal eating. This produces a fear of the new experience of tasting and eating food, or the child may not have the proper skills to cope with the appropriate texture of food for his or her age (Douglas & Bryon, 1996).

RISK FACTORS

Although this area suffers from a lack of research, a few studies have been conducted investigating the risk factors for the development of childhood-onset eating problems. It is important to note that studies have looked at risk factors in terms of those that lead to eating problems in general, without focusing on risk factors that may lead to specific disorders.

Low birth weight

Butler & Golding (1986) in a longitudinal study of British children found that feeding difficulties are common in premature and low-birth-weight infants. To further support this finding, 22% of children referred to the pre-school eating problems clinic at Great Ormond Street Hospital had been born early (Douglas & Bryon, 1996).

Developmental delay

Over one-third of the children referred to the pre-school eating problems clinic at Great Ormond Street Hospital were found to exhibit a mild or severe delay in attaining motor milestones such as sitting, walking and toilet training. Nineteen per cent exhibited a mild delay and 10% a severe delay in language development (Douglas & Bryon, 1996).

Early onset of the feeding problem

Sixty-two per cent of mothers of children referred to the pre-school eating problems clinic at Great Ormond Street Hospital described distress on feeding in the first three months of life. Weaning had also proved to be a problem, with 60% of children refusing to eat pureed baby foods and 59% refusing textured baby food. A strong association between feeding problems occurring at 0–3 months and continuing into 3–6 months was found (Douglas & Bryon, 1996). In addition, Dahl & Sundelin (1992) found in their longitudinal study that 71% of four-year-olds with an eating problem had early refusal to eat at 3–12 months of age (food refusal).

History of frequent vomiting of long duration

Parents of children referred to the pre-school eating problems clinic at Great Ormond Street Hospital reported that 70% of the children had vomited regularly or frequently (Douglas & Bryon, 1996).

Gender

Within the child population, it has been observed that males form a greater proportion of those presenting with eating problems, compared with the proportion presenting in late adolescence or adulthood. Fosson *et al* (1987) carried out a study of 48 children with early-onset anorexia nervosa and found that 27% were male, and Higgs *et al* (1989) found that 30% of children meeting the criteria for anorexia nervosa in their study were male. In addition, Timimi *et al* (1997) found that two-thirds of the children with selective eating (extreme faddiness) in their study were boys. To put these figures into context, figures quoted for late adolescence and adult populations with eating disorders have typically been much lower – for example, the Eating Disorders Association states that between 5% and 10% of those with eating disorders are male.

Social class

It appears that the higher social classes are overrepresented in those who present for treatment of childhood-onset anorexia nervosa. Fosson *et al* (1987) reported that 46% of children included in their study were from the higher social classes. Higgs *et al* (1989) found that 54% of children presenting with anorexia nervosa were from a 'middle-class' background. It is important to note, however, that families from middle-class backgrounds may be more disposed to make use of the facilities open to them.

Cultural background

In the past, eating problems have more commonly been associated with people of White ethnic origin. However, they are now being reported in children from families who maintain their own beliefs and practices and socialise primarily with others from the same racial origin. Eating problems can no longer therefore be termed 'culture-bound'.

four intervention approaches

There is no one intervention approach for the treatment of childhood-onset eating problems – in fact a number of treatment approaches may be used and children may receive different treatments depending on their diagnosis and to which professional they present for treatment. However, children have a basic need no matter what their diagnosis "to be able to eat enough to grow and develop normally, and to find a way of addressing her/his emotional needs through a medium other than food" (Nicholls, 1999). Lask & Bryant-Waugh (2000) have highlighted a number of important requirements in treatment, shown in Box 4.1.

Box 4.1 Important requirements in treatment (for further information see Lask & Bryant-Waugh (2000) Anorexia Nervosa and Related Eating Disorders in Childhood and Adolescence)

- The clinician and parents need to agree about how to treat the child
- Information needs to be made available for parents and other family members
- Parents need to be involved in treatment
- Healthy eating patterns need to be re-established
- A healthy weight range needs to be worked out
- Family work and/or counselling for parents should be offered
- Individual therapy for the child should be offered
- Decisions about school need to be made
- If the child is of very low weight, then a decision needs to be made as to whether he or she needs to be taken into hospital

In practice, owing to the lack of services for children with eating problems, the treatment that is offered may be determined more by the professional background of the clinician to whom the child initially presents and the availability of resources than by the need of the child.

Treatments that may be offered are physical treatment, behavioural therapy, cognitive–behavioural therapy (CBT), individual psychodynamic psychotherapy, family therapy and parental counselling.

PHYSICAL TREATMENTS

Physical treatments are needed in only the more severe cases of eating problems such as childhood-onset anorexia nervosa. The basic aims of physical treatment are to initially re-hydrate the child and to treat nutritional deficiency in order to help the child to gain weight. Physical treatments that are of most value are the artificial feeding programmes such as naso-gastric feeding. This involves the passing of a narrow tube via the nose into the stomach. The child can then be fed via the tube with liquid food that is high in calories and nutrients. The use of medication is only of value where there are additional emotional problems such as depression or obsessionality.

BEHAVIOURAL THERAPY

Behavioural therapy is the most common treatment used when treating children of pre-school age. A number of behavioural treatment techniques are used. These can be divided into those addressing motivational problems and those addressing skill deficit problems.

Treatment of problems in motivation

Motivational problems focus on increasing appropriate behaviours or decreasing maladaptive behaviours. Behaviour that is appropriate needs to be increased where a child is capable of engaging in behaviour, but does not do so frequently enough. Positive reinforcement is used to increase the desired behaviour. The reinforcement is delivered immediately after every occurrence of the target behaviour. Once a high and stable rate of behaviour is achieved, then the frequency of reinforcement is decreased, so that the behaviour is maintained.

On the other hand, inappropriate behaviour needs to be decreased where a child is engaging in a behaviour to an excess. Five different methods may be used in order to reduce the frequency of this behaviour.

Antecedent manipulation

This process decreases the antecedents to the behaviour and so decreases the probability of it occurring. For example, children may be less likely to expel a food that they do not like if its taste is masked by a food that they do like.

Extinction

Here, the behaviour is decreased by terminating an ongoing contingency. For example, where parents terminate the meal when a child expels food, they must continue to feed. Initially, this would result in an increase in frequency of expulsion of food, which would then be followed by a decrease in frequency of expulsion of food and finally extinction of the behaviour.

Time out

This is where the child is removed from the positive reinforcement situation, which gives the child incentive to avoid removal and to earn return when removal occurs.

Differential reinforcement

Here, an extinction procedure is used to eliminate an excessive behaviour with positive reinforcement to introduce a more beneficial behaviour in its place.

Punishment

In this case, a consequence follows an undesirable behaviour in order to decrease its occurrence. The majority of the literature describes punishment in the form of noxious tastes such as lemon juice; however, contingent oral hygiene with mouthwash, over-correction, contingent restraint and contingent forced feeding are also used. It is important to point out that the use of punishment in emotionally damaged or distressed children has been questioned in terms of value and justification.

Treatment of skill acquisition deficits

Skill acquisition procedures teach the child to emit a new or more complex behaviour. These procedures include:

Shaping

This involves reducing a complex target behaviour into smaller components and then teaching and reinforcing these components until the target behaviour is acquired.

Prompting

This is used where a target behaviour occurs too infrequently for positive reinforcement. Prompts usually consist of instructions, gestures, or physical guidance given to increase the probability that a child will emit a behaviour, so that behaviour can then be reinforced. Once the behaviour occurs at a high and stable rate, then the prompts are gradually removed.

Modelling

This is used where a target behaviour occurs too infrequently for positive reinforcement, and requires that the child has imitation skills. The therapist instructs the child to 'do this' and then models a behaviour. The child is then given reinforcement if the imitation is a close approximation of the behaviour.

COGNITIVE–BEHAVIOURAL THERAPY

Cognitive–behavioural approaches to therapy are a particularly useful tool in the treatment of early-onset eating problems, especially for bulimia nervosa, selective eating (extreme faddiness) and functional dysphagia (food phobia).

Within CBT, the therapist helps the patient to examine and re-evaluate their dysfunctional thoughts that are causing the problematic eating behaviours and emotional responses. Therapy aims to achieve a change in behaviour along with a change in the way that the person thinks. The first goal of therapy is to understand how thoughts and feelings are associated with the environment. It is made clear how thoughts can influence the way that the person feels in a particular situation and which thoughts and feelings are produced by certain behaviours.

The cognitive–behavioural therapist will use different techniques in the treatment of children. For example, initially children need to be made aware that what they think about their world can affect how they feel and that they can think different things about the same situation, which will make them feel differently. In the treatment of adults, keeping a diary of their thoughts, behaviours and feelings forms an important part of therapy. This may be difficult for children to accomplish, however, so they are encouraged to keep cartoon diaries using pictures and thought and speech bubbles to record the most important events of their day. Other techniques that are adapted for the treatment of children include the use of board games with cards that contain uncompleted sentences about family, emotions, experiences and behaviour. This can help with the testing of hypotheses that were initially generated about the underlying issues of the eating problem. Another technique used is the 'Worry Bag' (Binnay & Wright, 1997), where the child is given a picture of an outline of a bag and encouraged to draw his or her worries inside it. This lets the child know that it is alright to have worries and makes them seem more real and manageable. Different worries can then be discussed at each session and problem-solving strategies used to resolve the worry, or tasks can be set to challenge the negative thoughts that the child has about what might happen.

Rewards play an important part in increasing desired behaviours. This can be done through the use of token charts. In the treatment of children, however, token charts may seem visually unrewarding. Therefore, pictures are used that form as the child is rewarded – for example, a caterpillar that increases in length or a flower that grows as petals are attached.

INDIVIDUAL PSYCHODYNAMIC PSYCHOTHERAPY

Psychodynamic psychotherapy is of particular use in the treatment of anorexia nervosa and FAED, but is also used to treat children with bulimia nervosa and pervasive refusal syndrome.

This is designed to enable the child to tolerate emotional experiences. The eating problem serves to enable the child to negotiate control and autonomy within his or her family. Treatment involves two family assessments in order to assess family strengths and weaknesses, and patterns of relating. An individual assessment is also carried out to ascertain the underlying pathology of the child. Ongoing parental or family work and individual therapy for the child is used. This contains equivalents of the parent–child relationship such as a focus on the child's inner and outer experiences, consistency of care-specific and defined boundaries and acceptance of the child, even when destructive or rejecting. A reliable and regular framework of meetings is agreed in order to allow the patient to develop trust in the therapist. The therapist must share the entire emotional experience of the child, empathising with as much of the child's inner feelings as he or she will allow. Therapy aims to help the child to experience being understood and accepted. Successful therapy involves the child taking responsibility for mothering him- or herself and being concerned about the feelings of others and forgiving parents.

FAMILY THERAPY AND PARENTAL COUNSELLING

This is the only therapeutic approach to have been shown to be particularly effective in the younger age group (Russell *et al*, 1987). It is not known, however, which components are crucial. Family therapy focuses on the family as a whole rather than on an individual. Aspects of family functioning that are looked at are the structural components, including the quality and effectiveness of parenting, quality of the marriage, degree of closeness or distance between children and their parents and the degree of protectiveness of the child with the eating disorder, patterns of communication, and a history of the family and what contributions from the past are relevant to the current problem.

The aim of family therapy is to enhance the quality of parenting by helping the couple to start working together rather than against each other and to identify and acknowledge problems and conflicts and find a means of resolving them.

The family may need help with communication problems, as communication may be in excess, non-congruent, deviant, displaced or inhibited. Family therapy aims to help families to communicate in a more constructive way and techniques will vary according to the type of dysfunction.

Overall family therapy enhances the competence of the parental sub-system, improves communication and links relevant aspects of the family history to the current problem.

TREATMENT OF SPECIFIC EATING PROBLEMS

Childhood-onset anorexia nervosa

When treating children with anorexia nervosa, it is important to make sure that parents and other family members have enough information and that they take charge of what is going on. An important decision that needs to be made is whether the child needs to be taken into hospital or not. Bryant-Waugh & Lask (1999) point out that taking the child into hospital would seriously be considered if any of the following were seen:

- The child's weight is less than 80% weight for height by age.

- The child has low blood pressure, slow pulse or poor circulation in the hands and feet.

- The child is constantly vomiting or vomiting blood, or there are signs of depression.

During treatment, it is important to calculate a weight that the child needs to reach. Also, the child will need a programme of re-feeding. Family and parental counselling are usually offered and individual therapy for the child. Decisions also need to be made about school.

Childhood-onset bulimia nervosa

The treatment of bulimia nervosa involves working out an eating pattern that the child can follow. This is so that bingeing and purging can be reduced. Family therapy and parental counselling and individual therapy for the child are offered, which give support and advice. Individual work carried out with the child is usually CBT and helps to identify what is happening, when it happens and what triggers the compulsions to binge and then purge. It also helps children to work out ways in which they can overcome these. Also, therapy helps children to look at the negative thoughts that they have about themselves and to re-evaluate these to increase self-esteem. In some cases, medication may need to be used to help to reduce the urge to binge, and if the child is also suffering from depression, then anti-depressants may be prescribed.

Selective eating/extreme faddiness

The main reason that children present for treatment for selective eating (extreme faddiness) is the social impact that the problem has as the child gets older and starts to socialise more. For these children, the selective eating (extreme faddiness) has no physical effects, so that they are healthy and growing normally. A combination of parental counselling and individual therapy is offered. The individual therapy helps children to try new foods and to decide which foods to try, how much of each new food to try, when and where they want to try it and who they want to be there. To begin with, the child will only try a very small amount of one food. It is important to take this at the pace of the child and so treatment is usually a slow process. Parental counselling helps parents and carers to be consistent in the way that they try and help the child and shows them how to support the child by using rewards and not forcing or punishing the child.

Restrictive eating/poor appetite

Generally, if the child is growing normally and is healthy, then there is no need to try and treat the restrictive eating (poor appetite) of the child. This is because the child's appetite will usually increase as the child gets older. This will be the case for the majority of children with restrictive eating (poor appetite). There is, however, a very small minority of children whose restrictive eating (poor appetite) is having an effect on their growth and health. In this case, the child would be taken into hospital for treatment. Sometimes, doing this and changing the child's environment is enough to make the child eat more. If this does not happen, however, and the child's health is still at risk and the child is very short, then growth hormones may be used, which will stimulate appetite and growth. It is important to note that these are only used as a last resort in treatment.

Food avoidance emotional disorder

The assessment and treatment of this eating problem are very similar to that for childhood-onset anorexia nervosa. The difference in the treatment of FAED is that the children usually have depression, anxiety or obsessive–compulsive symptoms as well. Medication to treat these symptoms is therefore more likely to be used. The medication prescribed can cause side-effects such as an upset stomach, feeling drowsy or having a dry mouth. These will usually disappear, however, after a week or two. Medication should not be used unless there are good reasons for doing so.

Functional dysphagia/food phobia

When deciding how to treat this problem, whether the child has a physical abnormality or not, a delay in growth and the specific fears that the child has about eating all need to be taken into account. This is because if the child has a physical problem, then this will need a specific type of treatment – for example, if the child has gastro-oesphageal reflux (see the Glossary, p. 61), then medication is used to speed up the emptying of the stomach. If the child has difficulty in swallowing, then speech therapy may help the child to overcome this. On the other hand, cognitive therapy is used to treat fears of taste, texture and vomiting, choking or suffocating. This usually helps the child to relax so that they are not so anxious. The cognitive techniques that are used will depend on how old the child is.

five long-term outlook

Outcome research is important so that more effective interventions may be developed and predictions can be made about the outlook of the different types of disorder. There is little information, however, about the prognosis and outcome of the early-onset eating problems. The majority of what we do know has come from clinical experience and expertise.

Problems in eating behaviour at this stage in the life course have a huge potential impact on the growth and development of the child. Babbitt *et al* (1994*b*) conducted a review in America of the behavioural assessment and treatment of paediatric eating problems and stated that the more severe cases of eating problems can place children at risk for severe weight loss, malnutrition, lethargy, impaired intellectual, emotional and academic development, growth retardation and even death.

OUTLOOK OF SPECIFIC EATING PROBLEMS

Childhood-onset anorexia nervosa

Childhood-onset anorexia nervosa is a difficult eating problem to overcome and probably the hardest of the childhood-onset eating problems to recover from. It also has the worst long-term outlook. According to Bryant-Waugh & Lask (1999), two-thirds of the children that suffer from anorexia nervosa make a good recovery, one-third partly recover, 5% remain unwell for a number of years and a small number will die. Death in children with anorexia nervosa is very rare and is usually a result of the consequences of starvation, the effects of continuous vomiting or suicide. Recovery for children with anorexia nervosa is very slow. Most of the physical effects owing to starvation seem to reverse when the children gain weight. Any long-term consequences can be treated.

Childhood-onset bulimia nervosa

If children who suffer from bulimia nervosa are treated by a specialist, then the outlook is quite good. It has been shown in adults that CBT is an effective treatment, as it helps the person to reduce bingeing and purging. It is thought that CBT is also a useful treatment for children, again to help them to eat normally and gradually stop bingeing and purging. Recovery will take time. Any long-term effects will be owing to the repeated vomiting and/or the use of laxatives, but these can be treated.

Selective eating/extreme faddiness

Children who suffer from selective eating (extreme faddiness) have a very good long-term outlook. By the time the children become teenagers, almost all of them will have grown out of selective eating. The children that do not grow out of it, which according to Bryant-Waugh & Lask (1999) is probably less than 1%, will continue to be selective eaters as adults. Selective eating does not seem to be such a problem to them, however, at this age. There are no known long-term consequences of selective eating regardless of whether the person has grown out of it or not.

Restrictive eating/poor appetite

Restrictive eaters do tend to be poor eaters throughout childhood, but have a good outlook. Their appetite seems to get bigger as they get older and by the time they are adults they are eating satisfactorily. Restrictive eaters grow into thin adults but they are not unhealthy. It is not unusual to find that one of the child's parents may have been similar when he or she was a child. Although these children are often of low weight, this does not seem to cause them any problems physically. They seem to have naturally small appetites and so remain healthy. If parents try to pressurise the child to eat more, this may cause the child long-term distress.

Food avoidance emotional disorder

There is not much information available about the long-term outlook of FAED. Treatment for this condition is similar to that for childhood-onset anorexia nervosa, and if this is followed and the additional emotional difficulties addressed, then these children do tend to make a good recovery. It seems likely that recovery will be slow, as with the other eating problems. Long-term problems may occur if the child was of a particularly low weight, had been pressurised into eating or the emotional problems had not been resolved.

Functional dysphagia/food phobia

This is a rare condition, so there is little information on the long-term outlook of this eating problem. It is a difficult condition to overcome, but there are not many adults who suffer from it, so it seems likely that most children grow out of it. If the child has a very limited diet and has lost a lot of weight, then complications may be similar to those found in children with anorexia nervosa. The child may also have ongoing psychological problems if he or she has been pressurised into eating.

EFFECT ON GROWTH AND DEVELOPMENT

Nutrition has a profound influence on children's growth and development. An adequate intake of carbohydrates, protein and other essential nutrients is required for the rapid growth and development of a young child. Dasha Nicholls and colleagues (unpublished research: further details available upon written request to D. Nicholls, Eating Disorders Team, Department of Psychological Medicine, Great Ormond Street Hospital for Sick Children, Great Ormond Street, London WC1N 3JH) conceptualise physical well-being in eating problems in terms of a scale ranging from normal to seriously ill. The scale ranges from normal weight, growth, development and eating patterns at one end to illness such as anorexia nervosa at the other, which affects all of these things. In between these two extremes, a number of disorders can be found. For example, with bulimia nervosa, which affects metabolic and hormonal functioning, eating patterns are disturbed and weight may be low, normal or high. In a child with selective eating (extreme faddiness), however, weight, growth and development are usually unaffected despite an extremely limited diet. FAED can be found closer on the scale to anorexia nervosa, as weight may be extremely low and this may have a serious impact on the growth and development of the child.

Physical assessment

Physical observation is important when assessing and treating children with eating problems in order to identify effects on growth and development. It is important to be able to identify when a body is starving and not thin but normal.

A comprehensive physical assessment should involve more than measuring height or weight in isolation. In order to monitor growth effectively, the following need to be taken into account:

- the availability of suitable growth charts;

- correct measurement techniques;

- the accurate transfer of measurements onto growth charts;

- correct interpretation; and

- access to specialist advice.

Physical assessment includes anthropometric measurements, which provide information on body muscle mass and fat reserves. The most commonly used measurements are body weight, height, triceps skin-fold, and mid-arm muscle circumference.

Body weight

Any child whose health or growth is causing concern should be weighed. Body mass index charts have been published and should facilitate the interpretation of weight for height, but further experience will be needed to determine their clinical value.

Height

The major influence on children's final height is genetic. They may be short simply because their parents are. Children's stature normally increases rapidly during the first two years of life and then gradually slows down to a sustained rate until puberty. There may be a slight acceleration, the mid-childhood growth spurt, between six and eight years of age. It is at puberty that their principal growth spurt occurs, after which growth is more or less completed.

The onset of eating problems before these phases of growth may have serious consequences in terms of the child's final height and bone density. Studies of growth in the atypical eating disorders such as selective eating (extreme faddiness) and FAED are in progress (further details available upon written request to D. Nicholls, Eating Disorders Team, Department of Psychological Medicine, Great Ormond Street Hospital for Sick Children, Great Ormond Street, London WC1N 3JH).

Skin-fold thickness

Skin-fold thickness measurements of the triceps and subscapular are useful when carried out repeatedly. They are of particular value in children who have nutritional problems, as they can predict whether children have a nutritional status appropriate for their length/height. Skin-fold thickness can also be used to predict the adolescent growth spurt, which is preceded by a loss of limb fat.

The long-term effects of malnourishment during childhood also need to be taken into account.

Growth curves

As a rule, if a child grows less than 4 cm in any year, then medical attention should be sought (see Appendix IV for details on how to fully assess a child's growth potential). Once it has been recognised that a child is not growing enough, a growth curve needs to be established. One measurement taken in isolation will not show whether a child's growth is normal or abnormal; a pattern needs to be established and this is called the growth curve. A second measurement is then taken 6–12 months after the initial measurement, and a third taken after a further 6–12 months. These will provide the necessary information to establish a growth curve. The curve should run parallel to the growth chart's centile lines.

Since 1993, new 'cross-sectional' growth charts for the UK have replaced the Tanner Whitehouse longitudinal charts, which were devised in the 1950s and 1960s. These nine-centile charts show that the growth of children today is significantly altered; the average height of a nine-year-old girl has increased by 2 cm and her weight has increased by 1 kg. The charts are available from The Child Growth Foundation (see Useful addresses, p. 62).

Guidelines have been proposed that enable the identification of slow-growing children (Joint Working Party on Child Health Surveillance; Hall, 1996). It is important to note, however, that the authors of these guidelines emphasise that these proposals have not been formally tested to determine whether they are useful and acceptable to primary health care teams and how well they would perform in terms of sensitivity, specificity and positive predictive scale (see Box 5.1).

Box 5.1 *Criteria for the identification and referral of slow-growing children*

The child's height falls to below the 0.4th centile line or outside his or her Target Centile Range (TCR).

Pre-school children (less than 5 years):
- Refer if the child's height crosses two channel widths between any pair of measurements.
- Review after a further year if the child's height crosses one or more channel widths, but less than two.

School-aged children (5–9 years):
- Refer if a child's height crosses one or more channels between any pair of measurements.
- Review after a further year if the height crosses half a channel width or more between any pair of measurements.

Physical effects

General physiology

Fat stores play an important part in the effects that starvation will have on the body. The fat composition of the body varies and is relatively low during childhood and usually at its peak during puberty. Eating problems that occur at an age of six or seven years therefore occur when the body is in short supply of energy reserves. When the body is deprived of food, it conserves energy. This is done by limiting energy supply and blood flow to non-essential organs. These areas include the limb peripheries, the stomach and gut, and the skin. This results in symptoms such as cold hands and feet, pale skin and weak pulses. The brain is the last organ to be affected by a fall in blood flow. The body will also breakdown tissue so that the energy necessary to sustain organ function is available.

A wide range of physical effects of not eating an adequate diet has been observed. Electrolyte abnormalities are commonly seen in anorexia nervosa and although no studies have investigated the other types of eating problems in children, in some of the disorders children can be as malnourished, so it seems reasonable to presume that findings relating to low body weight could equally apply. Electrolyte abnormalities have been found in 50% of adult patients with bulimia nervosa (Mitchel *et al*, 1983), and are described in association with compensatory behaviours (Mira *et al*, 1987). These lead to potassium depletion (hypokalaemia), which may result in cardiac arrhythmias and sudden death. No specific studies in children, however, have been described.

Glucose metabolism is erratic during starvation and low blood glucose levels may be found (Mira *et al*, 1987). There are relatively few mineral or vitamin deficiencies that are not readily corrected with treatment. Investigation using child samples is limited, however. No abnormality on full blood count is found in the majority of acutely underweight patients. Anaemia is usually mild when it occurs and is usually a result of iron deficiency (Sharpe & Freeman, 1993). Liver enzymes are usually raised (Halmi & Falk, 1981) and these changes usually reflect fatty infiltration of the liver associated with malnutrition. Studies have been performed in adults, although clinicians believe that results are also true for children.

Eating disorders have an important and widespread effect on endocrine function – for example, thyroid function is variable in individuals presenting with anorexia nervosa. These effects are important in terms of both short and long-term consequences. Endocrine abnormalities tend to normalise with treatment.

Sexual development

The age at which puberty begins is variable. The average age for boys is 12 years (identified by testicular enlargement and pubic hair) and 11.5 years for girls (identified by the onset of breast development). In boys the growth spurt occurs relatively late during puberty, whereas in girls it may begin before there are any other physical signs.

An inadequate diet may lead to pubertal delay or where puberty has started the patient presents with arrested development and/or regression in some aspects of puberty. Girls may therefore have primary amenorrhoea (periods have never started), or secondary amenorrhoea (where periods started but have subsequently stopped – unlikely in children under the age of 12 years). Both of these are a sign of endocrine dysfunction and the loss of adequate sex steroid production. Sex steroids are important for the development of healthy bones, growth and the development of secondary sexual characteristics and reproductive function.

Growth

Rate of growth for age is one of the most sensitive markers of illness in childhood; however, currently, there is little information about the expected growth patterns in childhood-onset eating disorders – this is particularly true for boys. One of the few studies that looked at early-onset anorexia nervosa (Danzinger *et al*, 1994) found that 13 patients had growth arrest for approximately

13 months prior to admission. Catch-up growth occurred in nine patients, two showed no catch-up growth and two did not complete treatment.

The fastest period of growth for girls occurs on average at the age of 11 years and for boys on average at the age of 15 years. Onset of eating problems before these ages in terms of growth and bone density may have serious consequences. Studies of growth in the atypical eating disorders such as selective eating (extreme faddiness) and FAED are in progress (further details available upon written request to D. Nicholls, Eating Disorders Team, Department of Psychological Medicine, Great Ormond Street Hospital for Sick Children, Great Ormond Street, London WC1N 3JH).

Bone density

Osteoporosis is defined as "a bone mineral density (BMD) of more than 2.5 standard deviations (SDs) below peak bone mass (T score) for gender". It is characterised by low bone mass and an increase in bone fragility – this leads to an increase in the risk of fracture. The disorder is one of the major concerns in long-term morbidity associated with eating disorders, particularly in children, as bone strength is developing during this time.

Certain factors have been identified as having an effect on bone density – these are genes, race, nutrition, body weight, sex steroids, growth hormone and exercise (Dhuper *et al*, 1990; Ott, 1991; Lloyd *et al*, 1992). Anorexia nervosa has an impact on the majority of these factors – treatment therefore needs to maximise bone mass, which can be done through weight restoration.

Finkelstein *et al* (1992) have shown that in boys with significant delay in puberty, bone density is reduced relative to normal men in later life. Bone density in males with anorexia nervosa has not specifically been studied, however.

The digestive tract

Gastro-intestinal symptoms are the most frequently reported by patients with eating disorders (Carney & Andersen, 1996); however, on examination there appears to be very little wrong and the symptoms generally resolve on re-feeding (Rigaud *et al*, 1988; Waldholtz & Andersen, 1990).

Superior mesenteric artery syndrome (SMA) may also occur in malnourished patients and is a result of compression of the third part of the duodenum and the nerves and vessels of the superior mesenteric bundle. This occurs as a result of the cushion of fat protecting the bundle being lost (Adson *et al*, 1997). SMA is characterised by chronic abdominal pain, feeling full after a meal and vomiting.

The heart

Starvation can result in bradycardia (pulse less than 60 beats per minute), which is thought to be a sign of cardiovascular compromise. The effect of prolonged starvation and strain on the heart can result in reduced cardiac muscle mass, increasing the likelihood of hypotension, peripheral oedema and arrhythmias.

The liver and kidneys

Low fluid intake, vomiting, and diuretic or purgative abuse may lead to dehydration and renal stones. Starvation may result in reduced muscle mass, which has been observed in one 16-year-old to cause renal failure (Wada *et al*, 1992). In addition, fatty infiltration of the liver is well recognised in kwashiorkor and other states of severe malnutrition.

The brain

Structural abnormalities have been noted on the brain scans of patients with anorexia nervosa. These abnormalities may be partially reversible on weight gain and in younger patients may be entirely so (Golden *et al*, 1996). However, the extent of the impact of anorexia nervosa or the other eating disorders of childhood on the developing brain is largely unknown.

The link between diet and cancer

No longitudinal research studies have been performed to examine the incidence of cancer in children who have had a very restricted diet. However, we do know that evidence of dietary protection against cancer is strongest and most consistent for diets that are high in fruit and vegetables (American Institute for Cancer Research and The World Cancer Research Fund , 1997). Diets high in vegetables and/or fruits protect against cancers of the mouth, pharynx, oesophagus, lungs (the evidence for this is strongest for green vegetables) stomach, colon and rectum.

The World Cancer Research Fund recommends that individuals eat five or more portions (servings) a day of a variety of fruit and vegetables, all year round.

outline of current service provision

DISCIPLINES INVOLVED

A number of disciplines may be involved in the assessment and treatment of children with early-onset eating problems.

Community practitioners

Feeding problems may first be uncovered through routine check-ups, management of acute illness or parental concern. The general practitioner or community paediatrician may address the problem directly or refer the child to a medical specialist – for example, a paediatric gastroenterologist to diagnose reflux or a radiologist to help characterise swallowing problems.

Nutrition

Paediatric dieticians evaluate a child's nutritional status, diet, parental knowledge of nutrition and details of family diet. They provide parental counselling and consult with other professionals. They may treat children with problems of metabolism or pulmonary disease, and paediatric burn patients, for example.

Psychology

Child psychologists design behavioural protocols and work with children and their families to improve the child–parent relationship and reduce the stress around feeding issues.

Health visitors

Health visitors are registered nurses who have been trained in a health prevention role. They work within the community as members of the primary health care team. They often assess and manage problems associated with behaviour, eating and sleep. They may also work with local child and adolescent mental health service (CAMHS) teams.

Nursing

Paediatric nurses often treat hospitalised infants and young children, and play an important part in monitoring the progress of feeding interventions. If the intervention is based in an out-patient setting, mental health nurses may provide counselling or service coordination and visiting nurses support in the home.

Psychiatry

Child and adolescent psychiatrists may be involved in assessing emotional and behavioural problems of children, young people and their families. In addition, they are able to identify other neurodevelopmental and genetically determined conditions.

Occupational therapy

Paediatric occupational therapists focus on the use of the upper extremities, positioning and teaching the child how to feed independently. They may work individually with the child, help parents promote independent feeding and may also function as a consultant.

Speech therapy

Paediatric speech and language therapists are specifically trained to evaluate oral–motor dysfunction and so would treat children with problems in oral–motor activity or swallowing.

Physiotherapy

Physiotherapists have training in gross motor development and functioning and so would treat children with, for example, cerebral palsy, who have significant neuromuscular impairment.

Social work

Social workers provide therapeutic services such as individual counselling for parents or family therapy, or secure and coordinate community services. They may also act as case managers on feeding teams.

Although each of the above professions offers special areas of expertise, there is often overlap in professional functioning. For example, oral–motor problems may be treated by a speech and language therapist or a physiotherapist. The professional treating the child will depend on the facility to which he or she was referred. It is recognised that effective evaluation and intervention requires multi-professional collaboration; however, there are no clinical standards or guidelines for determining which combination of professionals should treat a particular child. The professionals that do become involved depend on the nature and severity of the eating problem, the clinical resources available, the organisation of health care services within a facility and the community, and the theoretical perspectives and practice or those managing the case (Kedesdy & Budd, 1998).

SPECIALIST SERVICES

Children may not present initially to an eating disorder specialist. Fosson *et al* (1987) found that 52% of children presenting with determined food avoidance spent time on a general paediatric ward before referral to a child psychiatric team. The delay in referral has been linked to atypical presentation and a lack of awareness that these conditions can occur in boys (Jacobs & Isaacs, 1986; Fosson *et al*, 1987). In fact, at the present time there are very few specialist services that treat childhood-onset eating problems.

research within the field

HISTORY/BACKGROUND

Literature on all aspects of eating problems specifically relating to children is sparse, which may partly be because children with eating problems have been recognised as a subgroup only within the past 20 years. The area suffers from a lack of robust research, in that no systematic reviews or randomised controlled trials (RCTs; see below for definition) have been conducted.

Literature that is available has come from experts working in two established areas of research at each end of the spectrum of eating problems – that is, experts working in the area of anorexia nervosa, bulimia nervosa, etc. who have branched downwards in age and those working in the area of failure to thrive who have branched upwards in age.

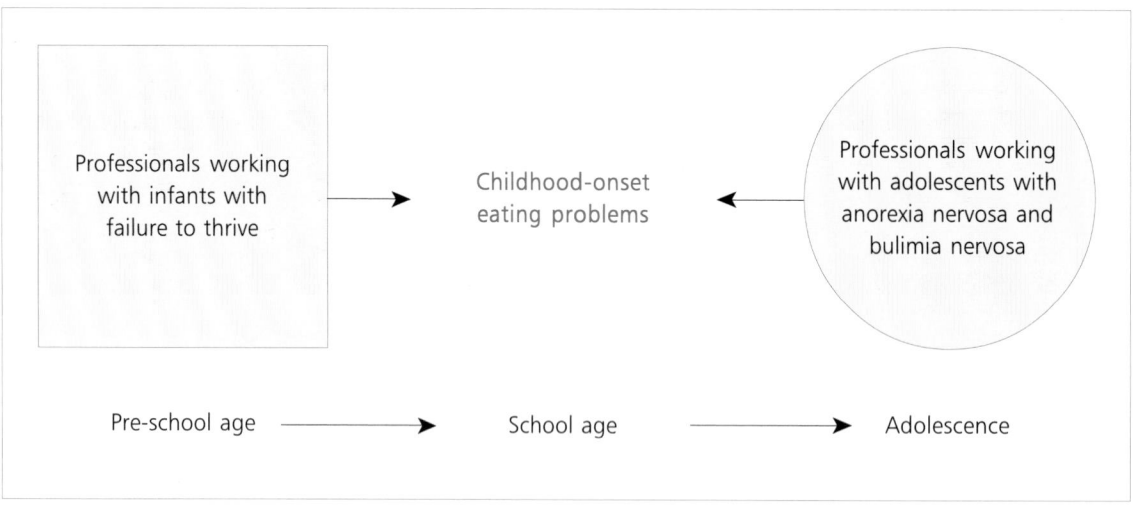

Fig. 7.1 Professionals treating school-age children with eating problems

QUANTITY AND QUALITY OF RESEARCH

Within an area of research a hierarchy of evidence exists:

(i) Systematic reviews
     This is the process by which studies are located and appraised, and evidence produced, so that it is possible to achieve a reliable overview of the research in question.

(ii)   Randomised controlled trials

In this type of experimental study design, subjects are randomly allocated into either a treatment group or a control group. Information relating to the effectiveness of the intervention is obtained through the comparison of the two groups.

(iii)   Cohort studies

A cohort design usually takes the form of a prospective epidemiological study in which two groups of individuals differ in their exposure to an intervention or hazard. The groups are then followed in order to assess the outcome and to estimate the strength of association between exposure and outcome. These studies can be conducted retrospectively, however.

(iv)   Case-control studies

These studies are usually retrospective in nature and are used to investigate the cause of disease. Subjects who have been affected by disease are compared with those who have not and differences in the presence or absence of hypothesised risk factors are recorded.

(v)   Case series

A case series is an uncontrolled observational study that involves an intervention and an outcome for more than one person.

(v)   Case studies

A case study is again an uncontrolled observational study that involves an intervention and an outcome, but for one person only.

(NHS Centre for Reviews and Dissemination, 1996)

In an ideal world, systematic reviews and RCTs will have been conducted within the field of interest. This is not always the case, however, and is certainly not true for the area of childhood-onset eating problems. The area suffers from a lack of robust research, with no systematic reviews or RCTs having been conducted. In fact, there is little research to be found on eating problems that specifically relates to children, in particular the 5–12-year-old age group. In addition, trying to identify the relevant literature that does exist is difficult in itself, mainly owing to the lack of standardised terms used to describe the different types of problems and the fact that there is no common classification system for the disorders.

OVERVIEW OF RESEARCH

The little research that has been conducted within the field has mostly concentrated on investigating the nature and outcome of the various disorders. In terms of study design, research has utilised case series or clinical case studies, neglecting more robust methodology.

Outcome studies in general have suffered from methodological flaws such as the use of small sample sizes, no comparison groups, failure to detail methods of sample selection (for example, through recruitment or clinical referral), inadequate follow-up and inadequate reporting of attrition rates. Few outcome studies, however, have investigated the outcome of the atypical early-onset eating problems – for example, selctive eating (extreme faddiness), FAED or restrictive eating (poor appetite) – and much debate remains. This is also true in relation to early-onset anorexia nervosa. Some authors believe that an early age of onset is associated with a poor prognosis (Dally, 1969; Swift, 1982; Bryant-Waugh *et al*, 1988; Bryant-Waugh *et al*, 1996), while others dismiss the prognostic significance of an early age of onset (Warren, 1968; Hawley, 1985; Jarman *et al*,

1991). Swift (1982) conducted a critical review of seven early-onset anorexia nervosa studies and concluded that there is insufficient evidence in the long-term outcome literature to support the statement that an early age of onset of anorexia nervosa is associated with a good outcome. Better outcome research is needed, in order to settle the debate about the prognostic significance of childhood-onset anorexia nervosa and to shed light on the outcome of the other eating problems found in children.

Longitudinal studies have found that experiencing an eating problem early on in life can have consequences on the child's future behaviour (Brandon, 1970), health (Hart *et al*, 1984), growth (Davis *et al*, 1978) and development (Brown & Matheny, 1971). In addition, children with early eating problems are more likely to continue to have a problem later on. For example, Dahl & Sundelin (1992) found that 71% of children with early refusal to eat still had an eating problem at the age of four years, with 42% reported to have behavioural problems. This was further followed into primary school age and indicated that early refusal to eat predicted more eating problems at home and at school (Dahl *et al*, 1994).

Risk factors that have been identified for the emergence of eating problems in children include maternal factors and infant-feeding behaviour and low body mass during the first month of life (Sanders *et al*, 1993; Stice *et al*, 1999). Lindberg *et al* (1994) found that food refusal is associated with weaning problems, less positive perceptions of parenting and infant difficulties and problematic behaviours. Environmental factors are also thought to play an important part in the development of eating problems in children, for example behavioural mismanagement during feeding (Iwata *et al*, 1982; Riordan *et al*, 1984) and adverse experiences such as ill health or tube feeding early in life (Geertsma *et al*, 1985; Skuse, 1985; Blackman & Nelson, 1987; Linscheid *et al*, 1987; Warady *et al*, 1990; Wittenburg, 1990; Budd *et al*, 1992).

Clinical profiles have highlighted that more boys suffer from eating problems within this age group than girls (Fosson *et al*, 1987; Timimi *et al*, 1997) and that children presenting with these problems generally represent the higher social classes (Fosson *et al*, 1987). In addition, case series and case studies have been important in identifying the different types of disorders experienced by the children within this age range. For example, Lask *et al* (1991) identified a syndrome characterised by a profound refusal to eat, drink, walk, talk or self-care with an aetiology of the trauma of sexual abuse. This was given further support by McGowan & Green in 1998. Research recognises that these eating problems in children have a complex aetiology (Koplow, 1993; Bryant-Waugh & Lask, 1995), and need multi-professional collaboration.

Research on the treatment of eating problems again is sparse and more often than not relies on case series and case study designs. Investigation into the treatment of food refusal has concentrated on the use of these clinical case studies or single-subject designs and the use of behavioural strategies (Werle *et al*, 1993). Behavioural parent training has been shown to increase offerings of food and the use of specific prompts and positive attention by mothers and to increase acceptance of foods and self-feeding in children (Werle *et al*, 1993; Turner *et al*, 1994). In terms of the other eating problems in children, some research suggests that the most effective treatment for early-onset anorexia nervosa is family therapy (Russell *et al*, 1987; Eisler *et al*, 1997). Other treatment approaches that have been found to be effective include hypno-behavioural techniques for children with dysphagia and food aversion (Culbert *et al*, 1996) and hypnotherapy teamed with systematic desensitisation for selective eating (extreme faddiness) (Bennett, 1994).

To conclude, the majority of what is known about childhood-onset eating problems has been obtained through clinical experience and expertise and not through evidence based on robust research. Although this is not ideal, it is not necessarily a bad thing at this time, as it provides a starting point at least. Much research is in progress , which will further develop our understanding of childhood-onset eating problems. More robust research in terms of RCTs needs to be conducted however, in order to establish an evidence base for current practice.

RESEARCH TABLES

A number of research papers have been identified through searching various databases (the search strategy used and databases searched can be found in Appendix I). A summary of research papers identified has been presented in tabular format entitled 'Table of status of research' on p. 32. Research studies included in the table have been grouped according to the type of study, for example studies investigating outcome, causation and clinical profiles. The table provides an overview of each of these studies, with brief comments on the strengths and weaknesses of papers that were critically appraised. Only papers with a cohort, case-control or case series design, were critically appraised (see Appendix II for Critical appraisal tools).

In addition, the table provides comments on the quality of each study. Quality was assessed using the critical appraisal tools in terms of the answers given to the questions asked. For example, when critically appraising a study with a case series design, seven questions were asked. The maximum points that a study with a case series design could score would be 14 points – this is because studies were allocated 2 points for a 'yes' answer, 1 point if the answer was 'can't tell' and 0 points for a 'no' answer. The allocation of points in this way enabled comparison between studies identified with a case series design. A similar method was used for studies with both case-control and cohort designs; however, a different allocation of points was needed. (For a breakdown of the method of point allocation for each of the study designs see Appendix III.)

A detailed breakdown of the critical appraisal of each paper is then provided, again in tabular format entitled 'Details of critical appraisal of studies' on p. 43, with papers grouped according to their study design, that is, cohort, case-control or case series.

It is possible to identify studies between tables by using the code assigned to each paper. For example, the first study in the 'Table of status of research' is Dahl & Sundelin (1992). This has been assigned the code of '1a' and is a case-control study. The detailed critical appraisal of this study can therefore be located under 'Case-control studies' in the section 'Details of critical appraisal of studies'. Codes run numerically and alphabetically.

TABLE OF STATUS OF RESEARCH

Outcome studies

Author and study	Date	Study type	Subject no./age	Outcomes measured	Principal outcomes	Comments on quality
Dahl & Sundelin **Feeding problems in an affluent society: follow-up at four years of age in children with early refusal to eat (1a)**	1992	Case-control study (follow-up)	24 RTE 36 control 2–4 years	Parent interview and medical records.	At four years, 71% with early RTE still had a feeding problem. 42% reported to have behavioural problems. There was no difference in health, growth and development between the two groups.	*Quality:* The study met six of the nine criteria, scoring14/18. *Problems:* Information on feeding and behaviour was obtained only from parents, so need to be aware of recall bias and limitations of human recall. *Strengths:* Children representative of population in the catchment area. All subjects were accounted for at follow-up and there was very low drop-out.
Dahl et al **Children with early refusal to eat: follow-up during primary school (1b)**	1994	Case-control study (follow-up)	18 RTE 240 control Primary school age	Information on school and home eating and behaviour was collected, along with health and growth data.	Early RTE predicted more eating problems at home and school later on.	*Quality:* The study met five of the nine criteria, scoring 13/16. *Problems:* Methods of selection are unclear, so need to keep in mind the possibility of selection bias. *Strengths:* The sample of children was representative. All children were accounted for at follow-up, although the drop-out rate had increased. Drop-outs were investigated so that results were not biased.
Higgs et al **Anorexia nervosa and food avoidance emotional disorder (1c)**	1989	Cohort (follow-up)	27 AN 23 FAED 22 disorder of emotions 7–16 years	Clinical and background information and parent and subject interview.	Early-onset AN has a similar nature, course and outcome come to adult AN. Tallness at presentation was associated with poor outcome. FAED children represent a middle group between AN and emotional disorder.	*Quality:* The study met eight of the 10 criteria, scoring 16/20. *Problems:* Only results from direct interviews were used for comparison at follow-up. *Strengths:* There were defined selection criteria for each group. Case notes were surveyed independently by two people unaware of each other's findings. Drop-outs did not lead to biased results.

RTE, refusal to eat ; AN, anorexia nervosa; FAED, food avoidance disorder

Author and study	Date	Study type	Subject no./age	Outcomes measured	Principal outcomes	Comments on quality	
Bryant-Waugh et al Long-term follow-up of patients with early-onset anorexia nervosa (1d)	1988	Cohort (follow-up)	30 early-onset AN 14–30 years	Information on weight, growth, menstrual state, eating behaviour, mental state, etc.	Outcome was good for 18, 10 had moderate/severe impairment and two died. Poor prognosis was associated with early age of onset (<11 years), depression during the illness and a disturbed family life.	*Quality:* *Problems:* *Strengths:*	The study met four of the 10 criteria, scoring 10/20. No information was given on methods of selection, so not clear whether selection bias was operating. The authors used defined diagnostic criteria. The results are comparable with earlier childhood-onset studies. There was a long mean follow-up period. A relatively large sample size was used.
Werle et al Treating chronic food refusal in young children: home-based parent training (1i)	1993	Case series	Three boys 21–54 months	Intervention: behavioural parent training programme. Sessions taped in home and used as training materials.	Training increased offerings of food and use of specific prompts for all three mothers. Two mothers showed increased levels of positive attention. Children showed an increase in acceptance of foods and self-feeding.	*Quality:* *Problems:* *Strengths:*	The study met five out of seven criteria, scoring 11/14. There was no long-term follow-up to investigate whether effects were maintained. Subjects did not enter the study at the same point in their disease. Sample was representative of standard users of the intervention. Criteria for inclusion were defined. Outcomes were assessed using objective criteria. Inter-observer agreement was obtained in the assessment of child and parent feeding behaviour.
Culbert et al Hypno-behavioural approaches for school-age children with dysphagia and food aversion: A case series (1l)	1996	Case series	Five 5, 7.5, 9. 5, 10 and 13.5 years	Intervention: hypno-behavioural approach. Improvement in eating problem.	Child-oriented self-management strategies (i.e. hypnosis, educational intervention and cognitive–behavioural suggestions) proved to be a successful treatment for children with functional dysphagia, globus hystericus, phagophobia and food aversion.	*Quality:* *Problems:* *Strengths:*	The study met two out of seven criteria, scoring 5/14. No objective measurement was used in assessing outcomes. Comparison was made only in so far as to say that the treatment was effective for all children. Sample was representative of standard users of the intervention.

AN, anorexia nervosa

Author and study	Date	Study type	Subject no./age	Outcomes measured	Principal outcomes	Comments on quality
Atkins et al A multimodal approach to functional dysphagia (1m)	1994	Case study	One 7 years	Intervention: Behavioural, family and play therapy with alprazolam. Improvement in eating problem.	Successful treatment of fuctional dysphagia with a multimodal approach – behavioural, family and play therapy with alprazolam.	N/A
Singer et al Cognitive–behavioural treatment of health-impairing food phobias in children (1n)	1992	Case series	Three boys 8, 6 and 7.5 years	Intervention: cognitive–behavioural treatment. Improvement in eating problem.	Intervention: cognitive–behavioural treatment (individual management, shaping, desensitisation, realxation training, education and cognitive restructuring) had a positive effect on overall calorific intake, weight gain, number of solid foods accepted, etc.	*Quality:* The study met five out of seven criteria, scoring 11/14. *Problems:* Methods of selection are unclear, and in particular whether these were random. *Strengths:* Sample was representative of standard users of the intervention within an in-patient psychiatric setting. Outcomes were measured using objective methods of assessment. Criteria for inclusion were used.
Bennett Treatment of an adolescent boy with eating difficulties using hynotherapy and systematic desensisation (1o)	1994	Case study	One 15 years	Intervention: hynotherapy and systematic de-sensitisation. Improvement in eating problem.	Hypnosis, using relaxation, visualisation and ego-strengthening, combined with systematic desensitisation, was successful in treating a long-standing eating difficulty.	N/A
Smolak & Levine Toward an empirical basis for primary prevention of eating problems with elementary school children (1p)	1994	Survey	187 1st–5th grade	Body esteem scale and children's sex role inventory.	Body shape was found not to be an important com-ponent of attractiveness. Children believed that weight could be affected by behaviour. Children who had tried to lose weight had lower body self-esteem scores.	N/A
Calam et al Eating attitudes in young teeange girls: parental management of 'fussy' eating (1q)	1997	Survey	92 11.0–13.11 years	Food management questionnaire, eating attitudes test, bulimic investigatory test.	Behavioural management techniques were ineffective. Parental modelling does not induce fussiness but may maintain it.	N/A

Author and study	Date	Study type	Subject no./age	Outcomes measured	Principal outcomes	Comments on quality	
Jarman et al **Late adolescent outcome of early onset anorexia nervosa** (1r)	1991	Cohort	43 girls Mean 18.3 years	Physical and menstrual state, eating behaviour, psychosocial and global outcomes measured.	Physical outcome was in normal range for 94% of girls at follow-up. Only 56% reported regular cyclical menstrual function. Only 25% had normal eating behaviour. Favourable physical outcome was found to be associated with higher premorbid and admission BMI percentiles, family history of obesity and shorter duration of illness on admission.	*Quality:* *Problems:* *Strengths:*	The study met five out of 10 criteria, scoring 10/20. Methods of selection are unclear. Details of diagnostic criteria used are not stated. Results only generalisable to other in-patient populations diagnosed with AN. All subjects were accounted for. Methods of follow-up were explained.
Bryant-Waugh et al **A propective follow-up of children with anorexia nervosa** (1s)	1996	Cohort	22 children 8.0–15.6 years	Information on weight and growth, menstrual state, eating behaviour, mental state and psychosocial and psychosexual adjustment obtained.	Long-term outcome was good in 10 (56.5%), intermediate in five (27.6%) and poor in three (16.7%). No children had died. Menstrual irregularities persisted in 46%, eating difficulties in 39%, and 72% obtained satisfactory psychosocial adjustment and 73% psychosexual adjustment. No prognostic factors were identified. Findings confirm unsatisfactory prognosis for this age group.	*Quality:* *Problems:* *Strengths:*	The study met five out of 10 criteria, scoring 10/20. Methods of selection are unclear. No comparison group is used. The results are comparable with earlier work. An adequate length of follow-up at a mean of 3.1 years was used.

AN, anorexia nervosa

Author and study	Date	Study type	Subject no./age	Outcomes measured	Principal outcomes	Comments on quality	
Hawley **The outcome of anorexia nervosa in younger subjects** (1w)	1985	Cohort (follow-up)	21 children <13 years	Information on height, weight, menstrual function, dietary pattern and attitudes toward food and body weight, sexual attitudes, family and social relationships, educational or occupational attainment and current psychiatric morbidity obtained.	No deaths occurred. Nutritional outcome was good in 12 cases (67%). Menstrual outcome was regular in nine (50%) and irregular in three. Disturbed eating behaviour was reported in eight out of the 18 cases. Occupational outcome was good for nine (50%), intermediate for six (33%) and poor for three (17%). Concluded that age at onset does not have prognostic significance.	*Quality:* *Problems:* *Strengths:*	The study met five out of 10 criteria, scoring 10/20. Methods of selction were not random. No comparison group was used. The study had a long mean period of follow-up. Drop-out was low. All subjects were accounted for at the time of follow-up.
Dahl & Sundelin **Early feeding problems in an affluent society. I Categories and clinical signs** (1x)	1986	Case-control study	50 infants 3–12 months	Feeding and behavioural characteristics, physical examination, mother behaviour and mother–child interaction, somatic health, weight development, growth data and psychosocial information.	Three main problem categories were identified: refusal to eat (28), colic (9) and vomiting (8). Problems had often begun at an early age and had persisted for a long time. Eight infants had significant medical disorders, which in seven explained the feeding problem. In 23 infants, the weight increase had been poor since the start of the feeding problem. Child health centre (CHC) nurses considered most of the problems troublesome, difficult to treat and uncommon.	*Quality:* *Problems:* *Strengths:*	The study met five out of nine criteria, scoring 14/18. The authors gave no details about the control group in this study. Observer bias was not controlled for. Sample was representative of standard users of the intervention. Data were obtained from various sources controlling for information bias.

Author and study	Date	Study type	Subject no./age	Outcomes measured	Principal outcomes	Comments on quality
Dahl *Early feeding problems in an affluent society.* III Follow-up at two years: natural course, health, behaviour and development (1y)	1987	Case-control study	42 feeding-problem children 42 controls 2 years	Feeding and behavioural characteristics, somatic health, utilisation of medical services, psycho-motor development, speech ability and psycho-social health.	In 21 (50%) of feeding-problem children, the problems persisted at the age of two years. There were significantly higher frequencies of infections and behavioural problems among these children than among controls. No differences in psycho-motor development were found. Recurrent infections and behavioural and psycho-social problems were significantly correlated with severe persistent feeding problems at two years of age.	*Quality:* The study met seven out of nine criteria, scoring 15/18. *Problems:* Little information was presented about methods of follow-up. Interviewer and observer bias was not controlled for. *Strengths:* The sample was taken from standard users of the intervention. Data were obtained from a variety of sources. Controls for comparison were taken from the same population and matched for age and gender.
Dahl & Kristiansson *Early feeding problems in an affluent society.* IV Impact on growth up to two years of age (1z)	1987	Case-control study	42 cases 42 controls 2 years	Growth data, weight and length measured.	After the onset of symptoms, the s.d scores of attained weight and length decreased significantly in children with refusal to eat and vomiting. The rate of weight gain was significantly lower in the refusal to eat group than in the control group. At two years of age, the children with vomiting had recovered and showed complete catch-up growth, while the refusal to eat group had attained significantly lower s.d. scores of attained weight and length than the control group. The risk of growth impairment was greatest in children who refused all food or all food except breast milk.	*Quality:* The study met seven out of nine criteria, scoring 15/18. *Problems:* Methods of selection were not random. The sample was taken from standard users of the intervention. Data were recorded regularly and in a standardised way. Drop-out was very low, details of which were given. *Strengths:*

Causation studies

Author and study	Date	Study type	Subject no./age	Outcomes measured	Principal outcomes	Comments on quality
Rydell et al **Characteristics of school children who are choosy eaters** (3a)	1995	Survey	240 6.1–11.0 years	Parental and teacher questionnaires, information on eating and general behaviour and information from health records.	Choosiness was found in one-third of the children, but only 8.5% were found to be choosy at home and at school. Choosy children had higher levels of problem behaviours. A history of RTE in infancy led to a more pronounced choosiness and problem behaviours.	N/A
Stice et al **Risk factors for the emergence of child-hood eating disturb-ances: a five-year prospective study** (3b)	1999	Cohort study	216 Infants	Information on BMI, sucking duration, parental weight, maternal eating behaviours and pathology, and childhood eating disturbance.	Risk of emergence of inhibited, secretive overeating and vomiting increased annually to the age of five years. Maternal factors predicted the emergence of child eating problems. Infant feeding behaviour and body mass during the first month of life were also predicting factors.	*Quality:* The study met five out of seven criteria, scoring 14/20. *Problems:* The measure used to assess childhood eating disturbance does not have established reliability and validity. *Strengths:* The use of multiple measures (direct, observational, etc.) reduced the risk that reporter bias or method variance accounted for the results. Attrition rates were low at 6.2%. The authors investigated drop-outs and found that they did not differ from those who completed the study, so the results were not biased as a result.

RTE, refusal to eat ; BMI, body mass index

Author and study	Date	Study type	Subject no./age	Outcomes measured	Principal outcomes	Comments on quality	
Lindberg et al **Early food refusal: infant and family charcteristics (3d)**	1994	Case-control study	23 in case group, 24 in control group Infants <18 months old	Information on feeding, family health, infant development, demographic variables, etc.	Infants with food refusal had lower relative weight at inclusion and at follow-up at two years. Food refusal was associated with weaning problems, parental reports of lower food consumption, higher frequency of meals, psycho-social problems in the family, less positive perceptions of parenting, infant difficulties and problematic behaviours.	*Quality:* *Problems:* *Strengths:*	The study met three out of nine criteria, scoring 9/18. Unclear where or how the control group was selected. Information was obtained from parents, without any back-up from records, so need to keep this in mind when interpreting the results. Overall, this paper makes very confusing reading. Well-defined inclusion and exclusion criteria for cases. Cases were identified through CHCs in Sweden, so children were representative of the catchment population.

CHC, child health centre

Clinical profiles

Author and study	Date	Study type	Subject no./age	Outcomes measured	Principal outcomes	Comments on quality	
Chatoor et al Food refusal after an incident of choking: a posttraumatic eating disorder (5a)	1988	Case series	Five 8, 9, 10, 10 and 11 years	Improvement in the eating problem	Treatment of food refusal owing to an incident of choking involved initially addressing nutritional needs, then anxiety through de-sensitisation and family therapy. Recovery was seen in all five children	*Quality:*	The study met five out of seven criteria, scoring 11/14
						Problems:	Outcomes were not measured using objective means of assessment. Selection procedures were not detailed, so it is unclear whether methods were random or not
						Strengths:	Cases entered the study at a similar point in their eating problem, all with a short history with a marked incident of choking. The sample was representative of standard users of the intervention
Koplow Musn't bite the hand that feeds: the boy who refused to eat (5b)	1993	Case study	One 9 years		The aetiology is complex and includes issues such as separation anxiety, diffuse boundaries between patient and mother and control. Need to identify multiple factors and address each for resolution of the problem	N/A	

Author and study	Date	Study type	Subject no./age	Outcomes measured	Principal outcomes	Comments on quality
McGowan & Green Pervasive refusal syndrome: a less severe variant with defined aetiology (5c)	1998	Case study	One 11 years		Pervasive refusal can exist as a spectrum disorder of varying severity. The case study gives support for the aetiology of sexual abuse and the post-traumatic nature of the syndrome described by Lask *et al* (1991).	N/A
Timimi et al Selective eaters: a retrospective case note study (5d)	1997	Case series	33 4–14 years	Demographic details, reason for referral, presenting symptoms including eating habits, developmental, psychiatric, family history and background, and outcome.	More than two-thirds were boys. A significant minority had poor growth or weight gain. Symptoms included anxiety, obsessive–compulsive symptoms, and social and school difficulties. Mealtimes were battles and a history of depression in at least one parent was found in one-third of couples.	*Quality:* The study met three out of seven criteria, scoring 8/14. *Problems:* The study is based on clinical case reports, so that the quality of the data obtained depends on the quality and accuracy of the records kept by the assessing and treating clinician. *Strengths:* The sample was taken from standard users of the intervention. In the selection of cases, two independent assessors were used to verify information obtained from the content analysis.
Nunn & Thompson The pervasive refusal syndrome. Learned helplessness and hopelessness (5e)	1996	Case study	One 15 years		Learned helplessness/hopelessness provides a useful model to understanding the aetiology and treatment of pervasive refusal.	N/A
Lask et al Children with pervasive refusal (5f)	1991	Case series	Four girls 9, 11, 13 and 14 years		Profound and pervasive refusal to eat, drink, walk, talk or self-care. Long-term treatment needed. Aetiology: (a) trauma of sexual abuse; (b) fear of family member, threats, consequences of disclosure.	*Quality:* The study met four out of seven criteria, scoring 9/14. *Problems:* Methods of selection were unclear. Objective methods of assessment were not used. *Strengths:* Sample was representative of standard users of the intervention. Comparison was made between cases and aetiological factors discussed.

41

Author and study	Date	Study type	Subject no./age	Outcomes measured	Principal outcomes	Comments on quality
Fosson et al Early onset anorexia nervosa (5h)	1987	Case series	48 children <14 years	Demographic features and clinical features including weight, height and nutritional state were measured and an assessment of family organisation and functioning performed.	A high proportion of cases were boys, much higher than in the adult population. Clinical features were similar in boys and girls. The sample was biased towards social classes I and II. Thirty (66%) achieved all their therapeutic goals, however nine failed to gain weight.	*Quality:* The study met five out of seven criteria, scoring 11/14. *Problems:* Methods of selection were not random. The authors used well-defined inclusion criteria. Agreement was achieved by multiple raters on diagnosis, giving the study added reliability. The sample was representative of standard users of the intervention. Inferential statistical comparison was made. *Strengths:*
Chatoor & Egan Non-organic failure to thrive and dwarfism due to food refusal: a separation disorder (5i)	1983	Case series	Nine cases 1–5 years	Case histories were identified for each child.	Children attempt to define themselves as a separate, autonomous being by refusing food, which involves the mother more deeply in the child's eating behaviour.	*Quality:* The study met one out of seven criteria, scoring 3/14. *Problems:* The study was not based on a random sample. Outcomes were not assessed using objective criteria. Comparison was not made between cases. *Strengths:* Sample was representative of standard users of the intervention.
Kent et al Pre-menarchal bulimia nervosa (5j)	1992	Case series	Six females 16–33 years	Continuity of bulimia nervosa into later life (no objective measurement used).	Pre-menarchal bulimia nervosa occurs much less commonly than early-onset anorexia nervosa.	*Quality:* The study met two out of seven criteria, scoring 5/14. *Problems:* Data collection method used human recall. The method of sampling used was not random. *Strengths:* Well-defined inclusion criteria were used. Diagnosis was confirmed by two independent clinicians. The sample was representative of standard users of the intervention.

DETAILS OF CRITICAL APPRAISAL OF STUDIES

Cohort studies (follow-up studies)

Title	**Anorexia nervosa and food avoidance emotional disorder** (1c)
Author/date	**Higgs *et al* (1989)**
Subject no./age	27 children with anorexia nervosa, 23 with FAED and 22 with a disorder of emotions; aged 7–16 years.
Setting	Children were recruited through the searching of all records from 1958 to 1984 from the Royal Manchester and Booth Hall Children's Hospitals.
Classification used	*Anorexia nervosa group:* Diagnostic criteria set out by Russell (1970) were modified to include only children in whom puberty was not complete and who exhibited behaviour that led to a marked loss in body weight or had a morbid fear of becoming fat, or had no signs of menarche in girls or secondary sexual characteristics in boys.
	FAED group: Disorder of emotions in which food avoidance is a prominent symptom; a history of food avoidance or difficulties such as food fads or restrictions lasting for at least one month; failure to meet the criteria for anorexia nervosa; an absence of organic brain disease, psychosis, illicit drug misuse or prescribed drug-related causes.
	Disorder of emotions group: Disorder of emotions in which the main symptoms include anxiety, together with degrees of panic and fearfulness. Other symptoms could be present, e.g. misery and sadness, obsessionality and hysterical phenomena.
Outcomes measured	Body weight and height, past medical and psychiatric history, including obstetric and peri-natal problems and past developmental difficulties, family adversities; e.g. medical and psychiatric histories and life events, demographic characteristics and social circumstances at the time of presentation were all taken from case notes.
Study design	Cohort study design – retrospective (to identify cases) and longitudinal study (follow-up).
Selection bias	Case notes were surveyed independently by two of the authors, who were unaware of each other's findings. Diagnosis was agreed by both.
Attrition bias	Methods of follow-up were well described; follow-up was only of the anorexia nervosa and FAED groups; details of follow-up (time, age of subjects, etc.) were given, two children from the FAED group died, two boys from the anorexia nervosa group were found to have a physical disease; 35 of 50 cases were interviewed, 13 refused a direct interview (26%) and data from a further six cases was obtained in another way. Loss at follow-up was therefore relatively low.
Results	Early-onset anorexia nervosa was found to be similar in nature, course and outcome to adult anorexia nervosa. Being tall at presentation was associated with a poorer outcome; FAED children seem to represent a middle group between the anorexia nervosa and emotional disorder groups.
Additional comments	The study puts forward a good case for the existence of early-onset anorexia nervosa and FAED. Drop-out does not seem to have biased the results; however, it is important to keep in mind that only results from direct interviews were used for comparison at follow-up.

Title	**Long-term follow-up of patients with early-onset anorexia nervosa** (1d)
Author/date	**Bryant-Waugh *et al* (1988)**
Subject no./age	30 children with early-onset anorexia nervosa; follow-up mean of 7.2 years; patients now 14–30 years of age.
Setting	Children presented at the Department of Psychological Medicine at Great Ormond Street Hospital.

Classification used	Children met the diagnostic criteria for anorexia nervosa as described by Fosson *et al* (1987).
Outcomes measured	Information on weight and growth, menstrual state, eating behaviour, mental, psychosocial and psychosexual states was obtained through patient interview or postal questionnaire (for six patients), general practitioner questionnaire and other questionnaires.
Study design	Cohort study design – long-term follow-up at mean age of 7.2 years, no controls used.
Selection bias	No information is given on methods of selection, so need to keep in mind that selection bias may have occurred.
Attrition bias	All subjects from the original study were accounted for; drop-out = 37.5%, but all those described and those who refused to participate (8.3% of the sample) were included in the analysis of outcome.
Results	Outcome was good for 18 (60%) of the sample, 10 had moderate to severe impairment and two children died. The authors conclude that a poor prognosis is associated with an early age at onset (<11 years), depression during the illness, a disturbed family life, one-parent families, and families where one or both parents had been married before.
Additional comments	The results are comparable with those of earlier childhood-onset studies. Also, the study had a long mean period of follow-up (7.2 years), and a relatively large sample size. However, methods of selection were neglected, so it is unclear whether the study was affected by selection bias.

Title	**Late adolescent outcome of early onset anorexia nervosa** (1r)
Author/date	**Jarman *et al* (1991)**
Subject no./age	43 adolescent girls who fulfilled diagnostic criteria for anorexia nervosa, aged 9–17 years (mean 14 years) on admission, follow-up at a mean of 4.3 years later (at a mean age of 18.3 years).
Setting	Girls had been admitted to the Royal Children's Hospital between 1977 and 1983 and underwent an in-patient treatment programme.
Classification used	The authors only state that children fulfilled "standard diagnostic criteria for anorexia nervosa"; it is unclear, however, whether these are DSM or ICD criteria.
Outcomes measured	Current physical, menstrual, eating behaviour, psychosocial and global outcomes were measured; this information was obtained from a physical examination, historical information psychiatric interview including the Offer Self Image Questionnaire (OSIQ; Offer *et al*, 1982), a self-report personality test and the Shaffer Global Assessment Scale (Shaffer *et al*, 1983).
Study design	Cohort study design with a long-term follow-up of subjects at a mean of 4.3 years later; no control group was used for comparison.
Selection bias	Subjects were admitted to the Royal Children's Hospital in Melbourne between May 1977 and May 1983; other than this no details are given on methods of selection, so need to keep in mind that selection bias may be operating.
Attrition bias	Of the 43 girls, only 32 presented for a follow-up interview, four could not attend for geographical reasons, three could not be contacted directly and the remaining three refused to attend or were prevented from doing so by their parents. Information on these 11 patients was obtained by phone interview and personal correspondence to find out if they significantly differed from non-drop-outs. Loss at follow-up was not an unreasonable amount and methods of follow-up were detailed; groups differed in that drop-outs were found to have a shorter duration of weight loss before admission and a more prevalent family history of anorexia nervosa.
Results	Physical outcome was within the normal range (3rd–97th percentiles) in 94% of the girls seen at follow-up; however, only 56% reported regular cyclical menstrual function (had all started menstrual periods at start of study as some were as young as nine

years? – this was not detailed by the authors); the majority were still dieting, bingeing or vomiting meals; psychosocial adjustment was satisfactory in the majority of cases, but varied widely. A favourable physical outcome was found to be associated with higher pre-morbid and admission BMI percentiles, family history of obesity and shorter duration of illness on admission.

Additional comments	Methods of selection are unclear and which diagnostic criteria were used, i.e. ICD or DSM. Analysis was conducted using only data from participants with drop-out data neglected. Differences were found between the two groups, so need to keep this in mind when interpreting the results.

Title	**A prospective follow-up of children with anorexia nervosa** (1s)
Author/date	**Bryant-Waugh *et al* (1996)**
Subject no./age	22 children with early-onset anorexia nervosa, 16 females and six males with an age range of 8.0–15.6 years.
Setting	Children presented for in-patient care at Great Ormond Street (GOS) Hospital.
Classification used	(a) Agreement to be followed up. (b) Treatment had been completed more than two years before the present follow-up study.
Outcomes measured	Information was obtained on weight and growth, menstrual state, eating behaviour, mental state and psychosocial and psychosexual adjustment. Information was gathered using semi-structured interviews, a postal questionnaire, a GP questionnaire, the GHQ (General Health Questionnaire; Goldberg & Miller, 1979), Eating Attitudes Test (Garner *et al*, 1982), and the GOS Depression Scale A; also parents completed the GOS Depression Scale B and the Rutter Scale A (Rutter *et al*, 1981). For children under the age of 16 years, the school teacher was also asked to complete a questionnaire. (GOS Depression scales are unpublished, but may be obtained upon written request to the Department of Psychological Medicine, GOS; see p. 62).
Study design	Cohort study design, a prospective follow-up of children with anorexia nervosa at a mean of 3.1 years, no control group was used for comparison.
Selection bias	No information was given on methods of selection, so need to keep in mind that selection bias may have occurred.
Attrition bias	Adequate follow-up was obtained for 18 of the 22 children – drop-out was therefore low. Methods of follow-up, however, were not detailed.
Results	Long-term outcome was good for 10 (55.5%) children, intermediate for five (27.8%) and poor for three (16.7%); no children had died; menstrual irregularities persisted in 46% and eating difficulties in 39%; psychosocial adjustment was obtained by 72% and 73% of the sample showed satisfactory psychosexual adjustment. No prognostic factors were identified. Findings support Bryant-Waugh *et al* (1988) and confirm the unsatisfactory prognosis for this younger age group.
Additional comments	The results are comparable with earlier work with an adequate follow-up period of a mean of 3.1 years. However, methods of selection are unclear, so it is unclear whether the study was affected by selection bias.

Title	**The outcome of anorexia nervosa in younger subjects** (1w)
Author/date	**Hawley (1985)**
Subject no./age	21 children with anorexia nervosa, aged 13 years or younger with a follow-up at a mean of 8.7 years later.
Setting	Subjects were referred to the Department of Psychiatry of Birmingham Children's Hospital between 1964 and 1982. The majority of the children required hospital admission, with only one child receiving out-patient care alone.

Classification used	All children met the DSM–III criteria for anorexia nervosa.
Outcomes measured	Height and weight, menstrual function, dietary pattern and attitudes toward food and body weight, sexual attitudes, family and social relationships, educational or occupational attainment and current psychiatric morbidity were all measured. Information was obtained from close relatives and from professionals, including family doctors and other psychiatrists; semi-structured interview techniques were also used.
Study design	Cohort study design with a follow-up at a mean of 8.7 years later.
Selection bias	Subjects were referred to the Department of Psychiatry at the Birmingham Children's hospital between 1964 and 1982. Most received in-patient care, with one receiving solely out-patient care. Selection seems to have been made on the bases of DSM–III and included all children referred during this time period under the age of 13 years, and therefore was not random.
Attrition bias	18 of the 21 cases were traced; two refused to be interviewed and one was living abroad. Brief details are given about methods of follow-up and drop-outs.
Results	No deaths had occurred; nutritional outcome was good in 12 cases (67%); menstrual outcome was regular in nine (60%) and irregular in three children; disturbed eating behaviour was reported in eight cases, with normal behaviour found in 10 children; occupational outcome was good for 13 subjects; psychosexual outcome, however, was poor; seven subjects were receiving continuing psychiatric care. The general psychological outcome measured found that nine (50%) had a good outcome, six (33%) intermediate and three (17%) a poor outcome. The authors conclude that age of onset does not have any prognostic significance.
Additional comments	The study has a long mean period of follow-up and a relatively large sample size. Results are similar to previous studies. Drop-out was low and all subjects were accounted for; drop-outs were not included in the analysis of results, but as drop-out was so low, this does not appear to have biased the results.

Title	**Risk factors for the emergence of childhood eating disturbances: A five-year prospective study** (3b)
Author/date	**Stice *et al* (1999)**
Subject no./age	216 newborn infants, 100 females and 116 males.
Setting	The infants were recruited from three hospitals in the San Francisco Bay area.
Classification used	(a) Born at term (<37 weeks gestational age).
	(b) Had APGAR (Apgar & Beck, 1972) scores of at least 7 at 1 and 5 minutes after delivery.
	(c) Had an absence of congenial abnormalities.
	(d) Did not experience any illness during their newborn hospitalisation.
Outcomes measured	Infant body mass, sucking duration, parental weight, maternal eating behaviours, maternal eating pathology and child eating disturbances were measured through laboratory assessment and a series of questionnaires, including the three-factor eating questionnaire and eating disorder inventory.
Study design	Cohort study – looking at the timing of onset of disturbed eating during childhood and the predictors of these behaviours.
Selection bias	Newborns and parents were recruited from the well newborn nurseries at a university hospital, a community hospital and a health maintenance organisation. Recruitment was performed by trained research assistants who first reviewed hospital records to identify eligible families. Mothers were then contacted in person at the newborn nurseries.
Attrition bias	Average annual attrition over the 5 years of the study was 6.2%. Authors looked at drop-outs and found that those with complete data did not differ significantly from

drop-outs on child gender, child body mass, child sucking duration, parental education, parental ethnicity, parental history of overweightness, maternal body mass, maternal restraint, maternal disinhibition, maternal hunger, drive for thinness, body dissatisfaction or maternal bulimic symptoms. The authors therefore conclude that attrition did not appear to have introduced systematic bias for any of the variables examined in the study.

Results	The risk of emergence of inhibited eating, secretive eating, overeating and vomiting increased annually to the age of five years. Maternal body dissatisfaction, internalisation of the thin ideal, dieting, bulimic symptoms and maternal and paternal body mass prospectively predicted the emergence of childhood eating disturbances. Infant feeding behaviour and body mass during the first month of life were also found to be predicting factors.
Additional comments	The measure used to assess childhood eating disturbance does not have established reliability and validity – however, the use of multiple data collection methods (direct measures, observational data, etc.) reduced the risk that reporter bias and method variance accounted for the findings. Attrition rates were low over the five-year period at 6.2%. Drop-outs were not significantly different from non-drop-outs, so results were not biased as a result of attrition.

Case-control studies

Title	**Feeding problems in an affluent society. follow-up at 4 years of age in children with early refusal to eat** (1a)
Author/date	**Dahl & Sundelin (1992)**
Subject no./age	24 children with refusal to eat, 38 control children; aged 2–4 years.
Setting	The population was recruited from children attending 10 child health care (CHC) units in Sweden. Cases had been previously investigated at 3–12 months of age for refusal to eat.
Classification used	(a) The infant should be aged between 3 and 12 months old.
	(b) Both parents and CHC nurses in agreement that the child presented with a feeding problem of some kind.
	(c) The feeding problem should have existed continuously without interruption for at least 1 month.
	(d) The primary help that had been given at the CHC should not have eliminated the problem.
Outcomes measured	Feeding and behaviour characteristics at four years, somatic health and medical care utilisation during the study period, speech and language evaluation, growth and psychosocial health at four years were all measured using parental interview, child health care units and medical records.
Study design	Case-control study – follow-up between 2 and 4 years of age of case children originally investigated at 3–12 months.
Selection bias	It is unclear whether the children were randomly assigned, so need to be aware of selection bias.
Control group	Controls were taken from the same child health care districts and matched individually with respect to age, gender and residential area.
Information bias	Information was taken from parents and backed up with information from the child health care units and reliable medical records; but information on feeding and behavioural characteristics was only obtained from parents.
Attrition bias	All subjects were accounted for; there was a very low drop-out rate – reasons for one case and one control were not known and three other controls were not traceable.

Results	At four years of age, 71% of the children with early refusal to eat still had a feeding problem; 42% were reported to have behavioural problems. No differences in health, growth and development were found between the two groups.
Additional comments	The sample was taken from child health care clinics in Sweden, which have almost 100% coverage in the country – so although a small sample size, the children were representative of the population in the catchment area. Parental interview only was used for data on feeding and behaviour, so recall bias and the limitations of human recall need to be taken into account. Results are consistent with previous studies. The risk of interviewer and observation bias, however, is still present.
Title	**Children with early refusal to eat: follow-up during primary school** (1b)
Author/date	**Dahl *et al* (1994)**
Subject no./age	18 children with refusal to eat; 240 control children; follow-up at primary school age.
Setting	The population was recruited from children attending 10 child health care clinics (CHCs) in Sweden previously investigated at 3–12 months of age (various follow-up studies have been done since this age).
Classification used	(a) The infant should be aged between three and 12 months old.
	(b) Both parents and CHC nurses in agreement that the child presented with a feeding problem of some kind.
	(c) The feeding problem should have existed continuously without interruption for at least 1 month.
	(d) The primary help that had been given at the CHC should not have eliminated the problem.
	Controls not to fulfil refusal to eat group criteria.
Outcomes measured	Eating and behavioural characteristics were investigated at home and at school by asking parents and teachers respectively; also, health and growth, occurrence and the nature of earlier feeding problems and certain socio-demographic variables were obtained from child health care units and school health records.
Study design	Case-control study – follow-up at primary school age of children originally investigated at 3–12 months (part of a longitudinal study).
Selection bias	Children were not randomly assigned – if they were, it was not explicitly stated, so need to be aware that selection bias may have occurred.
Control group	The control group consisted of current classmates of the refusal to eat group; these were recruited from grades 1–3, enrolled in 17 classes at 15 schools in rural, suburban, urban middle-class and urban working-class neighbourhoods. Parents of all 287 classmates were asked to participate – in the end, 240 parents agreed to participate details were given about reasons for non-response.
	No difference between age, gender, parental occupation, family constellation, sibling position, maternal age or social class of the family were found.
Information bias	Information was obtained from parents and teachers and backed up by child health care and school health records. Also, teachers were unaware of which children in their class had previously had a period of refusing to eat.
Attrition bias	All refusal to eat children were accounted for, seven dropped out owing to having moved too far away – these children apparently were not different from the other 18 in respect of gender distribution, psychosocial risk factors in family or previous disorders of health, growth and behaviour up to 4 years of age.
Results	Children who refused to eat at an early age presented with more eating problems both at home and at school compared with control children. No difference was observed in respect to general behaviour, somatic health or growth.

Additional comments	The sample of children used (cases and controls) was representative of the population. Although a different control group was used, differences were tested for on a number of variables and not found, so they were comparable. All children were accounted for at follow-up. Drop-outs increased in number but were not unreasonable and did not bias the results, as authors looked to see if drop-outs were different to non-drop outs – no difference was found. When interpreting results, need to keep in mind that (a) children's eating behaviour may vary from setting to setting; and (b) parents and teachers may experience the same behaviour differently.

Title	**Early feeding problems in an affluent society: I Categories and clinical signs** (1x)
Author/date	**Dahl & Sundelin (1986)**
Subject no./age	50 infants, 26 girls and 24 boys aged between 3 and 12 months, mean age of 7 months.
Setting	Population was recruited from children attending child health centres (CHCs) in Uppsala, Sweden. Data collection took place in three ways – by a visit to the infant's home, from various medical records and from interviews of the CHC nurses.
Classification used	(a) The infant should be aged between three and 12 months old.
	(b) Both parents and CHC nurses in agreement that the child presented with a feeding problem of some kind.
	(c) The feeding problem should have existed continuously without interruption for at least 1 month.
	(d) The primary help that had been given at the CHC should not have eliminated the problem.
Outcomes measured	Feeding and behavioural characteristics, infant previous and present state of health, physical examination, mother behaviour and mother–child interaction, somatic health and weight development, growth data and psychosocial health information. This information was obtained by a visit to the infant's home, from various medical records, including growth charts, and from interviews of CHC nurses.
Study design	Case-control study.
Selection bias	Children were not randomly assigned.
Control group	Details of controls are not given here – they are reported in later studies, however.
Information bias	Information was obtained from a variety of sources, in that data were obtained from parents and backed-up by medical records, a physical examination and questions to CHC nurses.
Results	Three main problem categories were distinguished: refusal to eat (28), colic (nine), and vomiting (eight). Problems had often begun at an early age and had persisted for a long time. Eight infants had significant medical disorders, which in seven of them explained the feeding disorder. In 23 infants, the weight increase had been poor since the start of the feeding problem. CHC nurses considered most of the problems troublesome, difficult to treat and uncommon.
Additional comments	The sample was taken from a population of standard users of the intervention. Data were obtained from a variety of sources to control for human recall. No details are given about the control group – these are reported in later studies.

Title	**Early feeding problems in an affluent society: III Follow-up at two years: natural course, health, behaviour and development** (1y)
Author/date	**Dahl (1987)**
Subject no./age	42 children with feeding problems, 23 girls and 19 boys aged approximately 2 years; 42 control children.

Setting	The population was recruited from children attending 10 child health centres (CHCs) in Uppsala, Sweden previously investigated at 3–12 months of age.
Classification used	(a) The infant should be aged between three and 12 months old (at initial investigation).
	(b) Both parents and CHC nurses in agreement that the child presented with a feeding problem of some kind.
	(c) The feeding problem should have existed continuously without interruption for at least 1 month.
	(d) The primary help that had been given at the CHC should not have eliminated the problem.
Outcomes measured	Feeding and behavioural characteristics, somatic health, utilisation of medical services, psychomotor development, including speech ability, psychosocial health. Data were obtained through interviews with parents in their homes (when child first enrolled, three months after first interview and at approximately 2 years), mealtime observation, physical examination, medical records, CHC records and interviews with CHC nurses.
Study design	Case-control study with a follow-up design of 2 years.
Selection bias	Children were not randomly assigned and the potential for selection bias not recognised.
Control group	Controls were taken from the same CHC districts as cases and matched pair-wise with respect to gender and age.
Information bias	Information was obtained from a variety of sources to control for information bias, in that data were obtained from parents and backed up using medical records, physical examination and questions to CHC nurses.
Attrition bias	All subjects were accounted for – no drop-out rate was stated and no details given.
Results	In 21 (50%) of the children with feeding problems, the problems persisted at the age of two years. There were significantly higher frequencies of infections and behavioural problems among the children with early feeding problems than among the controls. No differences in psychomotor development were found. Recurrent infections, behavioural problems and psychosocial problems were significantly correlated with severe persistent feeding problems at two years of age.
Additional comments	The sample was taken from standard users of the intervention. Data were obtained from a variety of sources to control for biases in human recall. Controls used for comparison were taken from the same population and were of the same gender and age.

Title	**Early feeding problems in an affluent society: IV Impact on growth up to two years of age** (1z)
Author/date	**Dahl & Kristiansson (1987)**
Subject no./age	42 children, 23 girls and 19 boys with a feeding problem aged 3–12 months on entry; 42 control children, 23 girls and 19 boys.
Setting	The population was recruited from children attending child health centres (CHCs) in Uppsala, Sweden.
Classification used	(a) The infant should be aged between three and 12 months old.
	(b) Both parents and CHC nurses in agreement that the child presented with a feeding problem of some kind.
	(c) The feeding problem should have existed continuously without interruption for at least 1 month.
	(d) The primary help that had been given at the CHC should not have eliminated the problem.

Outcomes measured	Growth data, weight and length were measured regularly under standardised conditions.
Study design	Case-control study with a follow-up design at 2 years.
Selection bias	Children were not randomly selected.
Control group	Controls were taken from the same CHC districts as cases and matched pair-wise for age, gender and residential area.
Information bias	Information was obtained from a variety of sources to control for information bias.
Attrition bias	All subjects were accounted for. One drop-out occurred where the child had moved abroad.
Results	After the onset of symptoms, the s.d. scores of attained weight and length decreased significantly in children with refusal to eat and vomiting. The rate of weight gain was significantly lower in the refusal to eat group than in the control group. At two years of age, the children with vomiting had recovered and showed complete catch-up growth, while the refusal to eat group had attained significantly lower s.d. scores of attained weight and length than the control group. It was found that the risk of growth impairment was greatest in children who refused all food or all food except breast milk.
Additional comments	The sample was taken from a population of standard users of the intervention. Data were obtained regularly and in a standardised way. Drop-out was very low, with only one girl who had moved abroad; children were not randomly assigned, however.

Title	**Early food refusal: infant and family characteristics** (3d)
Author/date	**Lindberg *et al* (1994)**
Subject no./age	23 cases with early refusal to eat, 24 controls; infants <18 months.
Setting	Infants were recruited from two parent questionnaire studies in the urban district of Uppsala, Sweden and from child health care (CHC) units, through reports from nurses about relevant infants.
Classification used	*Inclusion criteria:*

(a) There must be agreement between parents and the physician in the research project that the infant behaviourally refused offered food.

(b) Food refusal to occur at least once a day and the condition lasting for at least one month.

(c) Infant below the age of 18 months at inclusion.

(d) Full-term pregnancy with a birth weight of greater than 2 500 g and a gestational age of at least 37 weeks.

(e) Mother able to communicate in Swedish or English.

Exclusion criteria:

(a) Serious pre- or peri-natal complications, other than food refusal.

(b) Signs of significant organic causes for food refusal identified by hospital examinations and lab tests.

Outcomes measured	Information about physical growth, feeding characteristics, demographic characteristics, health characteristics, perceptions of parenting, infant difficultness and problematic behaviours were obtained through parental interview and observation.
Study design	Case-control study – using a longitudinal design and follow-up at two years of age.
Selection bias	Infants were recruited through two parent questionnaire studies and from CHC units. Selection was therefore on the basis of parental and nurse reports – 11 children were included from parents and 13 from nurse reports within the case group.

Control group	It is not clear how the control group was identified and from what population. They were matched to cases with regard to age, gender and CHC unit affiliation; individual matching was used.
Information bias	Information was obtained from parents (and authors when observing), which needs to be kept in mind when interpreting the results.
Attrition bias	All families were accounted for at follow-up. Drop-out was low: for questions regarding problem behaviours, 44/47 families were interviewed at two years – two case families and one control had moved away; and for questions regarding infant temperament one out of 44 families from the control group did not return the questionnaire.
Results	Infants with food refusal had lower relative weight at inclusion and at follow-up at two years. Food refusal was also associated with weaning problems, parental reports of lower food consumption, higher incidence of breast-feeding, a higher frequency of meals, psychosocial problems within the family, less positive perceptions of parenting, infant difficulties and problematic behaviours.
Additional comments	It is not made clear where the control group were selected from or how, but they were matched to cases. Information was obtained from parents, so need to keep in mind the limitations of human recall – no back-up with medical records was used. Nurses from CHC units identified separate cases, so there was no back-up here either. Attrition was low, however, and all families were accounted for. Overall, this paper makes very confusing reading!

Case series

Title	**Treating chronic food refusal in young children: home-based parent training (1i)**
Author/date	**Werle et al (1993)**
Subject no./age	Three boys aged between 21 and 54 months (1 year 9 months to 4 years 6 months), all with selective food refusal.
Setting	Subjects were referred by an out-patient psychology clinic in Chicago. All assessment and training was carried out in the kitchen area of the families' homes.
Classification used	(a) All three boys had been referred for chronic selective food refusal.
	(b) There was no medical explanation for the feeding problem.
	(c) Selective feeding problems had persisted for 15–50 months.
	(d) Each parent reported having virtually given up trying to feed the child non-preferred foods.
	(e) Children were developmentally capable of independent self-feeding (i.e. using fingers, spoon, fork and cup) and were able to follow simple directions.
	(f) None of the children were significantly underweight.
	(g) All came from middle-class, two-parent families and had no siblings with feeding problems.
Outcomes measured	Feeding observation coded 12 parent and seven child behaviours, seven food groups eaten and six food textures eaten. A typical meal-time was observed and videotaped, then coded. Behavioural parent training was then introduced using the videotapes. Once completed, observation took place again and so on.
Study design	Case series – evaluation of the effects of a behavioural parent-training programme on parent and child feeding-related behaviours in the home.
Selection bias	Children were recruited because they had been referred to an out-patient clinic in suburban Chicago for chronic selective food refusal. Methods of selection did not state that randomised techniques had been used, but the sample is representative

of standard users of the intervention. Children did not enter the study at a similar point in their disease.

Results	Training increased offerings of target foods and the use of specific prompts for all three mothers. Two mothers showed an increase in levels of positive attention. All three children increased acceptance of target foods and self-eating. The authors conclude that the results demonstrate the functional effects of parent training on in-home meal-times.
Additional comments	Children were representative of standard users of the intervention. Inter-observer agreement was obtained for child and parent behavioural observation, giving increased reliability to the study. There was no follow-up of subjects, however, to investigate whether effects were maintained. Outcomes were measured using objective methods.
Title	**Hypno-behavioural approaches for school-age children with dysphagia and food aversion: A case series** (1l)
Author/date	**Culbert *et al* (1996)**
Subject no./age	Five children, four boys and one girl; ages 6, 7.5, 9.5, 10 and 13.5 years; suffering from functional dysphagia, globus hystericus, conditioned fear of eating (phagophobia) and food aversion.
Setting	The paper describes five children treated for various maladaptive eating behaviours presented for treatment.
Classification used	Disorders associated with the act of swallowing: • Functional dysphagia – subjective description by patient or difficulty or discomfort associated with the act of swallowing that is not primarily owing to an organic medical problem. Disorders not associated with the act of swallowing: • Globus hystericus – the sensation of a 'lump in the throat' associated with nervousness or anxiety. • Phagophobia – a conditioned 'fear of eating' relating to concerns about gagging/choking/vomiting. • Food aversion/selectivity/refusal – avoidance or refusal of certain foods or liquids; these symptoms may or may not also be accompanied by the experience of nausea/vomiting on exposure to a non-preferred substance.
Outcomes measured	Outcomes were not measured objectively; the authors simply looked for an improvement in each child's condition.
Study design	Case series – presentation of five case studies with children with different diagnoses all treated using a hypno-behavioural approach.
Selection bias	It is unclear how subjects were selected as no information was given on this at all; it is therefore unknown if children were randomly selected. However, children had presented for treatment, so were representative of standard users of the intervention.
Results	Child-oriented self-management strategies, including hypnosis, educational interventions and cognitive–behavioural suggestions, provide a successful treatment for children with functional dysphagia, globus hystericus, phagophobia or food aversion.
Additional comments	The sample is representative of standard users of the intervention. Individuals did not enter the study at similar points in their eating problems; comparison that is made is only in so far as to say that the treatment was effective for all children. No objective measurement was used when assessing outcomes; however, the authors do state that the purpose of the paper was to stimulate interest and further exploration of eating behaviours in school-age children – which it should do.

Title	**Cognitive–behavioural treatment of health-impairing food phobias in children** (1n)
Author/date	**Singer et al (1992)**
Subject no./age	Three boys aged 6, 7.5 and 8 years; all suffering from severe dietary restriction and/or refusal to eat solid food.
Setting	All patients were admitted to the medical–behavioural centre (MBC) (a specialised in-patient psychiatric unit) for treatment of eating and other psychophysiological disorders.
Classification used	All patients had been hospitalised because of weight loss and malnutrition caused by severe dietary restriction and/or refusal to eat solid food.
Outcomes measured	Overall caloric intake, weight gain, number of solid foods accepted and the incidence of emesis were measured through medical, dietary, physical and speech therapy evaluations. Also, individual psychological assessment (using psychometric tests), baseline assessment of meals and a family assessment were carried out.
Study design	Case series – looking at cognitive–behavioural treatment of health-impairing food phobias in children.
Selection bias	All patients had been admitted to an in-patient psychiatric unit for treatment of eating and other psychophysiological disorders; it is unclear how individual cases were selected, so it is not known if selection was random or not.
Results	Cognitive–behavioural treatment, consisting of individual management, shaping, desensitisation, relaxation training, education and cognitive restructuring, had a positive effect on overall caloric intake, weight gain, number of solid foods accepted and incidence of emesis. Also, boys were found to be of average intelligence without other significant psychological or medical disorders; their eating disturbances were conceptualised as phobic disorders maintained by family factors reinforcing the children's avoidant behaviours.
Additional comments	The sample was representative of standard users of the intervention within an in-patient psychiatric setting – results may not be generalisable further than this population. Outcomes were measured using objective methods of assessment, standardised across cases. Criteria for inclusion were used, although one child had a short history of disease and the other two had long histories of similar duration. It is unclear how cases were selected and whether methods used were random; comparison was made between the three cases presented.

Title	**Food refusal after an incident of choking: A posttraumatic eating disorder** (5a)
Author/date	**Chatoor et al (1988a)**
Subject no./age	Five children, three girls and two boys; aged 8, 9 10, 10 and 11 years; all presenting with food refusal.
Setting	Subjects presented at a major paediatric hospital.
Classification used	Children presented with food refusal following an incident of choking, after which all children showed an acute onset of anxiety about the ingestion of food and associated refusal to eat.
Outcomes measured	Outcomes were not measured objectively – the authors simply looked at whether there was an improvement in the eating problem of the children.
Study design	Case series – reviewing five cases of food refusal after episodes of choking.
Selection bias	All children had presented to a major paediatric hospital for food refusal after an incident of choking. It is unclear how individual subjects were selected, so it is unclear whether methods used were random.
Results	Food refusal was the leading symptom after an incident of choking. Treatment involved initially addressing nutritional needs and then the child's anxiety through de-sensitisation; family therapy was then used to address the familial context in

which the disorder developed. Recovery was achieved for all five children (varying lengths of time taken), the majority needing additional treatment to address concurrent psychopathology.

Additional comments	All cases entered the study at a similar point in their eating problem; all had a short history with a marked incident of choking that was followed by food refusal. Selection procedures were not detailed, so it is unclear whether or not methods were random. Outcomes were not measured using objective means of assessment; however, a comparison of cases was made, including detailed discussion. The sample was representative of standard users of the intervention.

Title	**Selective eaters: a retrospective case note study** (5d)
Author/date	**Timimi *et al* (1997)**
Subject no./age	33 children, 24 boys and nine girls with selective eating; aged between 4 and 14 years.
Setting	Children had been referred to an under-8's feeding problems clinic or an over-8's eating-disorders team.
Classification used	Children were between the ages of 4 and 14, with a clear history of selective eating. Those with a medical condition that had caused feeding difficulties from an early age were excluded.
Outcomes measured	Demographic details, reason for referral, presenting symptoms including eating habits, developmental history, psychiatric history, family history and background, and outcome were all obtained from the database of the two clinics (six files were examined twice by two different people, independently, to verify that the same information was being collected using the content analysis method).
Study design	Case series – retrospective investigation of a number of cases of selective eating.
Selection bias	All children were identified from a database of two clinical teams (one under-eights and the other over-eights); all cases of selective eating were identified from the previous four years.
Results	Over two-thirds of the children were boys. A significant minority had poor growth or weight gain. The children suffered from anxiety, obsessive–compulsive symptoms, both food and non-food related, and often had social and school difficulties. Meal-times provoked anxiety that led them to turn into 'battlegrounds'. A history of depression was found in at least one parent in one-third of couples.
Additional comments	In the selection of cases, two independent assessors were used to verify information obtained from the content analysis. The study, however, is based on clinical case reports, so the quality of the data depends entirely on the quality and accuracy of the clinical records kept by the assessing and treating clinician. As no standardised research instruments were being used, it is difficult to compare the recorded information accurately. Subjects are representative of standard users of the intervention and the paper provides an insight into the characteristics and surrounding factors associated with selective eating.

Title	**Children with pervasive refusal** (5f)
Author/date	**Lask *et al* (1991)**
Subject no./age	Four children all girls; aged 9, 11, 13 and 14 years, all with pervasive refusal syndrome
Setting	Children had presented at the Department of Psychological Medicine at Great Ormond Street Hospital and did not fit into any existing diagnostic categories.
Classification used	Children had a profound and pervasive life-threatening condition manifested by a dramatic social withdrawal and determined refusal to walk, talk, eat, drink or care for themselves in any way for several months. The children had no organic disease.

Outcomes measured	Outcomes were not measured objectively – the authors purely look at whether there is an improvement after treatment. The condition and possible aetiological factors are detailed in the paper.
Study design	Case series – presenting four cases of pervasive refusal syndrome, a condition that did not fit into existing diagnostic criteria.
Selection bias	Methods of selection are unclear, so it is not known if they were random. Children presented to the Department of Psychological Medicine at Great Ormond Street Hospital.
Results	Characteristics of the syndrome are a profound and pervasive refusal to walk, talk, eat, drink or self-care in any way over a period of several months. Long-term and highly skilled nursing and psychiatric care is required to help these children to recover. In terms of aetiology, they propose a two-stage process:

(a) trauma of sexual abuse
(b) fear induced by family member/threats/consequences of disclosure.

Additional comments	The children were standard users of the intervention and so are representative of that population. Methods of selection were unclear and objective methods of assessment were not used. The authors put forward a good case for pervasive refusal syndrome, a condition that did not fit diagnostic criteria at that time; in addition, comparison is made between cases and aetiological factors discussed.

Title	**Early onset anorexia nervosa (5h)**
Author/date	**Fosson et al (1987)**
Subject no./age	48 children aged 14 years or younger with anorexia nervosa.
Setting	Children had been referred to the Department of Psychological Medicine at Great Ormond Street Hospital.
Classification used	Criteria used for diagnosis of anorexia nervosa were modified from Morgan & Russell (1975):

(a) determined food avoidance
(b) weight loss or failure to gain weight during the period of pre-adolescent accelerated growth (10–14 years) in the absence of any physical or mental illness
(c) any two or more of the following:

    (i) preoccupation with body weight
    (ii) preoccupation with energy intake
    (iii) distorted body image
    (iv) fear of fatness
    (v) self-induced vomiting
    (vi) extensive exercising
    (vii) purging (laxative abuse).

Outcomes measured	Demographic features and clinical features such as weight, height nutritional state, etc. were measured and an assessment of family organisation and functioning.
Study design	Case series describing 48 cases of early-onset anorexia nervosa.
Results	A high proportion of cases were boys, much higher than in the adult population. However, the clinical features were the same in both boys and girls. The sample were biased towards social classes I and II compared with the general population; 30 (68%) achieved all their therapeutic goals, 35 (80%) gained significant weight but fell short in one or more psychosocial areas and nine patients failed to gain weight.
Additional comments	The authors use well-defined inclusion criteria and identify cases using professionals from psychiatry and psychology with coded review forms and operationalised definitions. Also, a subgroup of files was reviewed by multiple raters with 0.93 concordance adding reliability to the study. Subjects were also representative of

standard users of the intervention. Although data were descriptive, inferential statistical comparison was made.

Title	**Non-organic failure to thrive and dwarfism due to food refusal: a separation disorder** (5i)
Author/date	**Chatoor & Egan (1983)**
Subject no./age	Nine cases – four boys and five girls aged between 1 and 5 years.
Setting	Children presented for treatment, no details given.
Classification used	No criteria stated.
Outcomes measured	Case histories were identified for each child to identify the course of the problem.
Study design	Case series.
Results	The authors conclude that the child attempts to define himself as a separate, autonomous being by refusing food, which involves the mother more deeply in the child's eating behaviour. The child wants to separate from the mother but is frightened to do so, so refuses to eat and ignores hunger pangs to get more attention from the mother.
Additional comments	The study is not based on a random sample. Outcomes were not assessed using objective criteria and comparison was not made between cases.

Title	**Pre-menarchal bulimia nervosa** (5j)
Author/date	**Kent *et al* (1992)**
Subject no./age	Six patients with a history of pre-menarchal binge eating, all female, now aged between 16 and 33 years.
Setting	Patients attended a bulimia clinic at St George's Hospital between 1980 and 1989.
Classification used	All patients met DSM–III criteria and subsequently DSM–III–R criteria for bulimia nervosa.
Outcomes measured	No objective measurement techniques were used. Looked at the relative frequency with which pre-menarchal bulimia nervosa might be expected to occur in a population of children.
Study design	Case series.
Selection bias	Methods of selection were not random; subjects were identified through all of the patients attending a bulimia clinic at St George's Hospital between 1980 and 1989. Each patient was seen twice by a different person to confirm the diagnosis, adding reliability to the study.
Results	The authors conclude that bulimia nervosa with an early age of onset occurs much less commonly than early-onset anorexia nervosa.
Additional comments	Clear and well-defined diagnostic criteria are used, and diagnosis was confirmed by two independent clinicians, adding reliability to the study. The major methodological shortcoming of the study is the method of data collection, that is, the use of human recall raises issues about its accuracy. In addition, a random sampling method was not used. Patients were, however, taken from a population of standard users of the intervention.

RECENT RESEARCH

Bryan Lask and colleagues are investigating how the atypical eating problems found in childhood differ from childhood-onset anorexia nervosa (research submitted for publication: further details available upon written request to B. Lask, Department of Psychiatry, Jenner Wing, St George's Hospital Medical School, Cranmer Terrace, London SW17 0RE; e-mail: b.lask@sghms.ac.uk). This research arose because it had been noted that in the adult population half of the eating-disorder patients seen fall into the DSM–IV (APA, 1994) 'eating disorder not otherwise specified' (EDNOS) group, in that they do not have full-blown anorexia nervosa or bulimia nervosa. In the child population, this EDNOS group looked very different to the typical eating-disorder groups. Other descriptive labels had therefore been given to the conditions that these children were suffering from. Children who took part in the study were aged between seven and 12 years. The study aimed to confirm the difference in psychopathology of these subtypes of childhood eating problems from childhood-onset anorexia nervosa. The results indicate that the research has in fact confirmed a difference in psychopathology. At the time of writing, papers and results are just coming out. Two papers have been written – one has already been submitted and the other one is about to be.

In addition, Nicholls and colleagues are investigating the growth and development aspect of childhood-onset eating problems, looking at whether diagnosis has any effect on the long-term outcome (further details available upon written request to D. Nicholls, Eating Disorders Team, Department of Psychological Medicine, Great Ormond Street Hospital for Sick Children, Great Ormond Street, London WC1N 3JH).

eight conclusions and recommendations

KEY ISSUES

There are three issues that stand out within the field:

1. Classification and research

Children with eating problems have only emerged as a subgroup of interest within the past two decades. The area has developed through experts working in two established areas of research at each end of the age spectrum – that is, those working in the area of eating disorders in adolescence, treating children with anorexia nervosa, etc., branching downwards in age, and those working in the area of feeding problems in infancy and early childhood, treating children who are failing to thrive, branching upwards in age. As a consequence, there is no formal classification system for childhood-onset eating problems. Neither of the two main diagnostic manuals, the ICD–10 (WHO, 1992) or the DSM–IV (APA, 1994), offers appropriate diagnostic categories for the types of problems experienced within this age range. The lack of an established classification system has meant that literature on all aspects of eating problems that specifically relates to children is sparse, so that the area suffers from a lack of robust research. Particularly neglected in terms of research are children in the 5–12-year-old age group presenting with the atypical eating problems such as selective eating (extreme faddiness), restrictive eating (poor appetite) and FAED.

2. Language and types of disorder

The second issue is one of language. The names of the types of disorders found are purely descriptive and have arisen from those working in the field out of a need for a language to describe the problems that the children that they treat are experiencing. In addition, the names of the different types of disorder tend to vary depending on the profession and background of the clinician. For example, selective eating may be termed 'extreme faddiness' or 'faddy eating' and restrictive eating as 'poor appetite'. A more standardised language is therefore needed, which can be obtained through the development of a classification system.

3. Current service availability

The last major issue that stands out within this field is the lack of current specialist service availability. Current specialist service seems to be limited to two hospitals, both of which are based in London. The first is Great Ormond Street Hospital (see Useful addresses, p. 62), which offers treatment for children between the ages of one and 15 years in two distinct clinics divided arbitrarily by age – pre-school and school-age. The second is Springfield University Hospital (see Useful addresses, p. 62), which treats children between the ages of seven and 14 years. A large number of professionals from varying backgrounds may be involved in the assessment and treatment of these children. The type of treatment received will often depend on which professional the child initially presents to.

WHAT ABOUT THE FUTURE?

There appear to be a lot of gaps within the literature that need to be addressed in the future. Much of the current research utilises case series and case study designs. In order to move on within the field in terms of research, more robust study designs are needed for the effective investigation of childhood-onset eating problems – this is particularly important for the 5–12-year-old age group and the atypical eating problems.

More specifically...

- The development of a comprehensive classification system for the problems found within the 5–12-year-old age group is required in order to assist research and the comparison of studies.

- Investigation into the aetiology of the different types of disorder is needed.

- Research evidence is required in order to support clinical practice in terms of the use of effective intervention approaches.

- Longitudinal research needs to investigate the long-term outlook for the individual disorders.

- More evaluation of current service is required in order to identify best practice.

- In terms of the debate regarding the long-term outcome of early-onset anorexia nervosa, RCTs would be of use to address this issue.

glossary

Aetiology	The study of the causes of disease.
Binge/bingeing	Eating within a limited period of time a larger amount of food than most individuals would eat under similar circumstances.
Cognition	A broad term that has been traditionally used to refer to activities such as thinking, conceiving, reasoning, problem-solving, etc.
Cognitive development	This refers to the sequence of changes that occur to the cognition of a person as they mature.
Conditioned response	This is any response that is learned or altered by conditioning.
Electrolytes	An electrolyte is a solution or a substance in solution that consists of various chemicals that can carry electric charges. Electrolytes can be found in the blood as acids, bases and salts, for example sodium, calcium, potassium and magnesium.
Endocrine	Endocrine system refers to glands that secrete hormones internally. Their secretions are distributed through the body via the bloodstream.
Enzymes	An enzyme is an organic catalyst that produces chemical changes in other substances without being changed itself.
Gastro-oesophageal reflux	This refers to a condition where the gastric contents of the stomach return to the oesophagus. Sometimes, gastric contents return to the pharynx and cause regurgitation and vomiting.
Hypotension	This is a term used to describe abnormally low blood pressure.
Incidence	The number of new cases of an event or a condition in a population in a given period.
Maladaptive	This literally means that which is not adaptive (not appropriate, useful or aiding in adjustment).
Naso-gastric feeding	This involves passing a narrow tube into the stomach via the nose. Feeding then occurs via the tube with specially prepared liquid food high in calories and nutrients.
Prevalence	This is the total number of cases of a disease or a disorder in a specified population at a particular point in time.
Psychopathology	This is the scientific study of mental disorders.
Purge/purging	To eliminate gastrointestinal tract contents by either inducing vomiting or laxative misuse.

The Child Growth Foundation
2 Mayfield Avenue
Chiswick
London W4 1PW
Tel: 020 8994 7625

The Children's Society
The Edward Rudolf House
69–85 Margery Street
London WC1X 0JL
Tel: 020 7841 4400

Department of Psychological Medicine (children
2–15 years of age)
Great Ormond Street Hospital for Sick Children
Great Ormond Street
London WC1N 3JH
Tel: 020 7405 9200

Eating Disorders Research Team (children 7–17
years of age)
Department of Psychiatry
Jenner Wing
St George's Hospital Medical School
Cranmer Terrace
London SW17 0RE
Tel: 020 8725 5514

Eating Disorders Service (children 7–17 years
of age)
Harewood House
Springfield University Hospital
Glenburnie Road
London SW17 7DJ
Tel: 020 8682 6751

National Children's Bureau
8 Wakely Street
London EC1V 7QE
Tel: 020 7843 6000

YoungMinds
102–108 Clerkenwell Road
London EC1M 5SA
Tel: 020 7336 8445

bibliography

Adson, D. E., Mitchell, J. E. & Trenkner, S. W. (1997) The superior mesenteric artery syndrome and acute gastric dilation in eating disorders: A report of two cases and review of the literature. *International Journal of Eating Disorders*, **21**, 103–114.

American Institute for Cancer Research and The World Cancer Research Fund (1997) *Food Nutrition and the Prevention of Cancer: A Global Perspective*. Washington, DC: American Institute for Cancer Research.

American Psychiatric Association (1994) *Diagnostic and Statistical Manual of Mental Disorders* (4th edn). Washington, DC: APA.

Apgar, V. & Beck, J. (1972) *Is My Baby All Right? A Guide to Birth Defects*. New York: Trident.

Archer, L. A. & Szatmari, P. (1990) Assessment and treatment of food aversion in a four year old boy: A multi-dimensional approach. *Canadian Journal of Psychiatry*, **35**, 501–505.

Arvedson, J. C. (1997) Behavioural issues and implications with paediatric feeding disorders. *Seminars in Speech and Language*, **18**, 51–69.

Atkins, D. L., Lundy, M. S. & Pumariega, A. J. (1994) A multimodal approach to functional dysphagia. *Journal of the American Academy of Child and Adolescent Psychiatry*, **33**, 1012–1016.

Babbitt, R. L., Hoch, T. A., Coe, D. A., *et al* (1994*a*) Behavioural assessment and treatment of paediatric feeding disorders. *Journal of Developmental and Behavioural Paediatrics*, **15**, 278–291.

—, — & — (1994*b*) Behavioural feeding disorders. In *Disorders of Feeding and Swallowing in Infants and Children* (eds D. N. Tuchman & R. S. Walter), pp. 77–95. San Diego, CA: Singular.

Baer, M. T. (1997) Nutrition services for children with disabilities and chronic illness. In *Mosby's Resource Guide to Children with Disabilities and Chronic Illness* (eds H. M. Wallace, R. F. Biehl, J. C. MacQueen, *et al*). St Louis, MO: Mosby.

Bennett, C. (1994) Treatment of an adolescent boy with eating difficulties using hypnotherapy and systematic desensitization. *Contemporary Hypnosis*, **11**, 33–36.

Binnay, V. & Wright, S. (1997) The bag of feelings: An ideographic technique for the assessment and exploration of feelings in children and adolescents. *Clinical Child Psychology and Psychiatry*, **2**, 449–462.

Blackman, J. A. & Nelson, C. L. A. (1987) Rapid introduction of oral feedings for tube fed patients. *Developmental Behavioral Pediatrics*, **8**, 63–67.

Boddy, H. M. & Skuse, D. H. (1994) Annotation: The process of parenting in failure to thrive. *Journal of Child Psychology and Psychiatry*, **35**, 401–424.

Brandon, S. (1970) An epidemiological study of eating disturbances. *Journal of Psychosomatic Research*, **24**, 253–257.

Brown, A. & Matheny, A. (1971) Feeding problems and preschool intelligence scores: a study using the co-twin method. *American Journal of Clinical Nutrition*, **24**, 1207–1209.

Bryant-Waugh, R. & Lask, B. (1995) Eating disorders in children. *Journal of Child Psychology and Psychiatry and Allied Disciplines*, **36**, 191–202.

—— & —— (1999) *Eating Disorders: A Parent's Guide*. London: Penguin Books.

——, Knibbs, J., Fosson, A., *et al* (1988) Long-term follow-up of patients with early onset anorexia nervosa. *Archives of Disease in Childhood*, **63**, 5–9.

——, Lask, B., Shafron, R., *et al* (1992) Do doctors recognise eating disorders in children? *Archives of Disease in Childhood*, **67**, 114–118.

——, Hankins, M., Shafran, R., Lask, B., *et al* (1996) A prospective follow-up of children with anorexia nervosa. *Journal of Youth and Adolescence*, **24**, 431–437.

Budd, K. S., McGraw, T. E., Farbisz, R., *et al* (1992) Psychosocial concomitants of children's feeding disorders. *Journal of Pediatric Psychology*, **17**, 81–94.

Butler, N. R. & Golding, J. (1986) *From Birth to Five: A Study of Health and Behaviour of Britain's Five Year Olds*. London: Pergamon.

Calam, R., Waller, G., Cox, A., *et al* (1997) Eating attitudes in young teenage girls: parental management of 'fussy' eating. *Eating Disorders the Journal of Treatment and Prevention*, **5**, 29–40.

Candy, C. M. & Fee, V. E. (1998) Underlying dimensions and psychometric properties of the eating behaviours and body image test for preadolescent girls. *Journal of Clinical Child Psychology*, **27**, 117–127.

Carney, C. P. & Andersen, A. E. (1996) Eating disorders: Guide to medical evaluation and complications. *Psychiatric Clinics of North America*, **19**, 657.

Chatoor, I. (1989) Infantile anorexia nervosa: A developmental disorder of separation and individuation. *Journal of the American Academy of Psychoanalysis*, **17**, 43–64.

—— & Egan, J. (1983) Non-organic failure to thrive and dwarfism due to food refusal: a separation disorder. *Journal of the American Academy of Child Psychiatry*, **22**, 294–301.

——, Dickson, L., Schaeffer, S., *et al* (1985) A developmental classification of feeding disorders associated with failure to thrive: Diagnosis and treatment. In *New Direction in Failure to Thrive* (ed. D. Drotar), pp. 235–258. New York: Plenum.

——, Conley, C. & Dickson, L. (1988*a*) Food refusal after an incident of choking: a posttraumatic eating disorder. *Journal of the American Academy of Child and Adolescent Psychiatry*, **27**, 105–110.

——, Egan, J., Getson, P., *et al* (1988*b*) Mother infant interactions in infantile anorexia nervosa. *Journal of the American Academy of Child and Adolescent Psychiatry*, **27**, 535–540.

——, Kerzner, B., Zorc, I., *et al* (1992) Two-year-old twins refuse to eat: a multidisciplinary approach to diagnosis and treatment. *Infant Mental Health Journal*, **13**, 252–268.

——, Getson, P., Menveille, E., *et al* (1997*a*) A feeding scale for research and clinical practice to assess mother–infant interactions in the first three years of life. *Infant Mental Health Journal*, **18**, 76–91.

——, Hirsch, R. & Persinger, M. (1997*b*) Facilitating internal regulation of eating: a treatment model for infantile anorexia. *Infants and Young Children*, **9**, 12–22.

——, Hirsch, R., Ganiban, J., *et al* (1998) Diagnosing infantile anorexia: the observation of mother–infant interactions. *Journal of the American Academy of Child and Adolescent Psychiatry*, **37**, 959–967.

Collins, W. (1894) Anorexia nervosa. *Lancet*, I, 202–203.

Cooper, P. & Stein, A. (1992) *Monographs in Clinical Paediatrics: Feeding Problems and Eating Disorders in Children and Adolescents*. Berkshire: Harwood Academic Publishers.

——, Watkins, B., Bryant-Waugh, R. & Lask, B. (2000) *Academy of Eating Disorders 9th International Conference*. New York.

Culbert, A. P.. Kajander, R. L., Kohen, D. P., *et al* (1996) Hypnobehavioural approaches for school-age children with dysphagia and food aversion: A case series. *Developmental and Behavioural Paediatrics*, **17**, 335–341.

Dahl, M. (1987) Early Feeding Problems in an affluent society: III. Follow-up at two years: Natural course, behaviour and development. *Acta Paediatrica Scandinavica*, **76**, 872–880.

—— & Kristiansson, B. (1987) Early feeding problems in an affluent society: IV. Impact on growth up to two years of age. *Acta Paediatrica Scandinavica*, **76**, 881–888.

—— & Sundelin, C. (1986) Early feeding problems in an affluent society: I. Categories and clinical signs. *Acta Paediatrica Scandinavica*, **75**, 370–379.

—— & —— (1992) Feeding problems in an affluent society: follow up at 4 years of age of children with early refusal to eat. *Acta Paediatrica*, **81**, 575–579.

——, Eklund, G. & Sundelin, C. (1986) Early feeding problems in an affluent society: II. Determinants. *Acta Paediatrica Scandinavica*, **75**, 370–379.

——, Rydell, A. M. & Sundelin, C. (1994) Children with early refusal to eat: follow-up during primary school. *Acta Paediatrica*, **83**, 54–58.

Dally, P. (1969) *Anorexia Nervosa*. London: William Heinemann Medical Books.

Danzinger, Y., Mukamel, M., Zeharia, A., *et al* (1994) Stunting of growth in anorexia nervosa during the prepubertal and pubertal period. *Israeli Journal of Medical Science*, **30**, 581–584.

Davis, R., Apley, J., Fill, G., *et al* (1978) Diet and retarded growth. *British Medical Journal*, **1**, 539–542.

Delgado, S. V., Emde, R. N. & Pope, K. K. (1993) An atypical eating disorder in a 2 year old female. *Bulletin of the Menninger Clinic*, **57**, 242–251.

Dhuper, S., Warren, M. P., Brooks Gunn, J., *et al* (1990) Effects of hormonal status on bone density in adolescent girls. *Journal of Clinical Endocrinology Metabolism*, **71**, 1083–1088.

DiNicola, V., Roberts, N. & Oke, L. (1989) Eating and mood disorders in young children. *Psychiatric Clinics of North America*, **12**, 873–893.

Douglas, J. (1991a) Chronic and severe eating problems in young children. *Health Visitor*, **64**, 334–336.

—— (1991b) Psychologically based eating problems in young children. *Maternal and Child Health*, **16**, 251–253.

—— (1992) When your child won't eat. *Parents*, September, 38–42.

—— (1995a) Behavioural eating disorders in young children. *Current Pediatrics*, **5**, 39–42.

—— (1995b) Behavioural eating problems in young children. In *Nutrition in Child Health* (ed. P. Davies), pp. 155–164. London: Royal College of Physicians.

—— & Bryon, M. (1996) Interview data on severe behavioural eating difficulties in young children. *Archives of Disorders in Children*, **75**, 304–308.

Eisler, I., Dare, C. & Russell, G. (1997) Family and individual therapy in anorexia nervosa: a five year follow-up. *Archives of General Psychiatry*, **54**, 1025–1030.

Finkelstein, J. S., Neer, R. M., Beverly, M. D., *et al* (1992) Ostoepenia in men with a history of delayed puberty. *New England Journal of Medicine*, **326**, 600–604.

Fosson, A., Knibbs, J., Bryant-Waugh, R., *et al* (1987) Early onset anorexia nervosa. *Archives of Disease in Childhood*, **62**, 114–118.

Frank, D. A. & Drotar, D. (1994) Failure to thrive. In *Child Abuse: Medical Diagnosis and Management* (ed. R. M. Reece), pp. 298–324. Philadelphia: Lea & Febiger.

Garner, D., Olmstead, M., Bohr, Y., *et al* (1982) The Eating Disorders Attitude Test: Psychometric features and chronic features. *Psychological Medicine*, **12**, 871–878.

Geertsma, M. A., Hyams, J. S., Pelletier, J. M., *et al* (1985) Feeding resistance after parenteral hyperalimentation. *American Journal of Disorders in Childhood*, **139**, 255–256.

Goldberg, D. & Miller, V. (1979) A scaled version of the General Health Questionnaire. *Psychological Medicine*, **9**, 139–145.

Golden, N. H., Ashtari, M., Kohn, M. R., *et al* (1996) Reversibility of cerebral ventricular enlargement in anorexia nervosa, demonstrated by quantitative magnetic resonance imaging. *Journal of Pediatrics*, **128**, 296–301.

Greer, D. R., Dorow, L., Williams, G., *et al* (1991) Peer-mediated procedures to induce swallowing and food acceptance in young children. *Journal of Applied Behavioural Analysis*, **24**, 783–790.

Hall, D. (1996) *Health for All Children*. Report of the third joint working party on child health surveillance (3rd edn). Oxford: Oxford University Press.

Halmi, K. A. & Falk, J. R. (1981) Common physiological changes in anorexia nervosa. *International Journal of Eating Disorders*, **1**, 16–27.

Hampton, D. (1996) Resolving the feeding difficulties associated with non-organic failure to thrive. *Child Care, Health and Development*, **2**, 261–271.

Hart, H., Bax, M. & Jenkins, S. (1984) Health and Behaviour in Preschool Children. *Child Care Health and Development*, 10, 1-16.

Hawley, R. (1985) The outcome of anorexia nervosa in younger subjects. *British Journal of Psychiatry*, **146**, 657–660.

Higgs, J. F., Goodyer, I. M. & Birch, J. (1989) Anorexia nervosa and food avoidance emotional disorder. *Archives of Disease in Childhood*, **64**, 346–351.

Hoch, T., Babbitt, R. L., Coe, D. A, *et al* (1994) Contingency contacting. Combining positive reinforcement and escape extinction procedures to treat persistent food refusal. *Behavioural Modifications*, **18**, 106–128.

Hsu, L., Crisp, A. & Harding, B. (1979) Outcome of anorexia nervosa. *Lancet*, i, 61–65.

Iwata, B., Riordan, M., Wohl, M., *et al* (1982) Paediatric feeding disorders: Behavioural analysis and treatment. In *Failure to Thrive in Infancy and Early Childhood: A Multidisciplinary Team Approach* (ed. P. J. Accardo), pp. 297–329. Baltimore: University Park Press.

Jacobs, B. W. & Isaacs, S. (1986) Pre-pubertal anorexia nervosa: A restrospective controlled study. *Journal of Child Psychology and Psychiatry*, **27**, 237–250.

Jaffe, A. C., & Singer, L. T. (1989) Atypical eating disorders in young children. *International Journal of Eating Disorders*, **8**, 575–582.

Jarman, F. C., Rickards, W. S. & Hudson, I. L. (1991) Late adolescent outcome of early onset anorexia nervosa. *Journal of Paediatric Child Health*, **27**, 221–227.

Kedesdy, J. H. & Budd, K. S. (1998) *Childhood Feeding Disorders: Behavioural Assessment and Intervention*. Baltimore, MD: Paul H. Brookes Publishing Co.

Kelly, C., Ricciardelli, L. A. & Clarke, J. D. (1999) Problem eating attitudes and behaviours in young children. *International Journal of Eating Disorders*, **25**, 281–286.

Kent, A., Lacey, H. & McCluskey, J. E. (1992) Pre-menarchal bulimia nervosa. *Journal of Psychosomatic Research*, **36**, 205–210.

Kerwin, M. E. & Berkowitz, R. I (1996) Feeding and eating disorders: ingestive problems of infancy, childhood, and adolescence. *School Psychology Review*, **25**, 316–328.

——, Ahearn, W. H., Eicher, P. S., *et al* (1995) The costs of eating: a behavioural economic analysis of food refusal. *Journal of Applied Behavioural Analysis*, **28**, 245–260.

Koplow, B. (1993) Mustn't bite the hand that feeds: the boy who refused to eat. *Journal of Child Psychotherapy*, **19**, 23–36.

Kramer, S. S. & Eicher, P. M. (1993) The evaluation of paediatric feeding abnormalities. *Dysphagia*, **8**, 215–224.

Kreipe, R., Churchill, B. & Strauss, J. (1989) Long-term outcome of adolescents with anorexia nervosa. *American Journal of Disorders in Childhood*, **143**, 1322–1327.

Kristiansson, B. & Fallstrom, S. P. (1981) Infants with low weight gain: II. Environmental factors. *Acta Paediatrica Scandinavica*, **70**, 663–668.

—— & —— (1987) Growth at the age of 4 years subsequent to early failure to thrive. *Child Abuse and Neglect*, **11**, 35–40.

——, Karlberg, J. & Fallstrom, S. P. (1981) Infants with low weight gain: I. A study of organic factors and growth patterns. *Acta Paediatrica Scandinavica*, **70**, 655–662.

Lask, B. & Bryant-Waugh, R. (1993) *Childhood Onset Anorexia Nervosa and Related Eating Disorders*. Hillsdale, NJ: Lawrence Erlbaum Associates.

—— & ——(2000) *Anorexia Nervosa and Related Eating Disorders in Childhood and Adolescence*. Hove: Psychology Press.

——, Britten, C., Kroll, L., *et al* (1991) Children with pervasive refusal. *Archives of Disease in Childhood*, **66**, 866–869.

——, Bryant-Waugh, R. & Gordon, I. (1997) Childhood-onset anorexia nervosa is a serious illness. *Annals of the New York Academy of Sciences*, **817**, 120–126.

Leung, A. K. & Robson, W. L. (1994) The toddler who does not eat. *American Family Physician*, **49**, 1789–1792, 1799–1800.

Lindberg, L., Bohlin, G. & Hagekull, B. (1994) Early food refusal: infant and family characteristics. *Infant Mental Health Journal*, **15**, 262–277.

Linscheid, T. R. (1992) Eating problems in children. In *Handbook of Clinical Child Psychology* (eds C. E. Walder & M. C. Roberts), pp. 451–473. 2nd edn. New York: John Wiley & Sons.

——, Tarnowski, K. J., Rasnake, L. K., *et al* (1987) Behavioural treatment of food refusal in a child with short gut syndrome. *Journal of Pediatric Psychology*, **12**, 451–459.

Lloyd, T., Rollings, N., Andon, M. B., *et al* (1992) Determinants of bone density in young women: I. Relationships among pubertal development, total body bone mass, and total body bone density in premenarchal females. *Journal of Clinical Metabolism*, **75**, 383–387.

McCallum, R. W., Grill, B. B., Lange, R., *et al* (1985) Definition of a gastric emptying abnormality in patients with anorexia nervosa. *Digestive Disease Science*, **30**, 713–722.

McGowan, R. & Green, J. (1998) Pervasive refusal syndrome: a less severe variant with defined aetiology. *Clinical Child Psychology and Psychiatry*, **3**, 583–589.

Magagna, J. & Nicholls, D. (1997) A group for the parents of children with eating disorders. *Clinical Child Psychology and Psychiatry*, **2**, 565–578.

Marshall, C. (1895) Fatal case in a girl of 11 years. *Lancet*, I, 817.

Mathisen, B., Skuse, D. & Reilly, S. (1989) Oral motor dysfunction and failure to thrive among inner city infants. *Developmental Medicine and Child Neurology*, **31**, 293–302.

Ministry of Agriculture Fisheries and Food (1997) *A Guide for Health Professionals Healthy Diets for Infants and Young Children*. London: MAFF.

Mira, M., Stewart, P. M., Vizzard, J., *et al* (1987) Biochemical abnormalities in anorexia nervosa and bulimia. *Annals of Clinical Biochemistry*, **24**, 29–35.

Mitchel, J. E., Pyle, R. L., Eckert, E. D., *et al* (1983) Electrolyte and other physiological abnormalities in patients with bulimia. *Psychological Medicine*, **13**, 273–278.

Morgan, H. & Russell, G. (1975) Values of family background and clinical features as predictors of long-term outcome in anorexia nervosa: Four year follow-up study of 41 patients. *Psychological Medicine*, **5**, 355–371.

Neilson, G. B., Lausch, B. & Thomsen, P. H. (1997) Three cases of severe early-onset eating disorder: Are they cases of anorexia nervosa? *Psychopathology*, **30**, 49–52.

Newman, M. M. & Halmi, D. A. (1988) The endocrinology of anorexia nervosa and bulimia nervosa. *Neurological Clinics*, **6**, 195–212.

NHS Centre for Reviews and Dissemination (1996) *Undertaking Systematic Reviews of Research on Effectiveness* (CRD Guidelines for those Carrying Out or Commissioning Reviews, CRD Report 4). York: NHS Centre for Reviews and Dissemination.

Nicholls, D. (1999) Eating disorders in children and adolescents. *Advances in Psychiatric Treatment*, **5**, 241–249.

Nunn, K. P. & Thompson, S. L. (1996) The pervasive refusal syndrome: Learned helplessness and hopelessness. *Clinical Child Psychology and Psychiatry*, **1**, 121–132.

O'Brien, S., Repp. A. C., Williams, G. E., *et al* (1991) Pediatric feeding disorders. *Behavior Modification*, **15**, 394–418.

Offer, D., Ostrov, E. & Howard, K. (1982) *Offer Self Image Questionnaire for Adolescents: A Manual*. Chicago, IL: University of Chicago Press.

Ott, S. M. (1991) Bone density in adolescents. *New England Journal of Medicine*, **325**, 1646–1647.

Palmer, R. & Treasure, J. (1999) Providing specialised services for anorexia nervosa. *British Journal of Psychiatry*, **175**, 306–309.

Patton, G. (1998) Mortality in eating disorders. *Psychological Medicine*, **18**, 947–951.

Perske, R. Clifton, A. McClean, B. M., *et al* (1977) *Mealtimes for Severely and Profoundly Handicapped Persons: New Concepts and Attitudes*. Baltimore, MA: Universal Park Press.

Ramsay, M., Gisel, E. G. & Boutry, M. (1993) Non-organic failure to thrive: Growth failure secondary to feeding-skills disorder. *Developmental Medicine and Child Neurology*, **35**, 285–297.

Richman, N., Stevenson, J. & Graham, P. (1982) *Pre-school to School: A Behavioural Study*. London: Academic Press.

Rigaud, D., Bedig, G., Merrouche, M., *et al* (1988) Delayed gastric emptying anorexia nervosa is improved by completion of a renutrition program. *Digestive Disease Science*, **33**, 919–925.

Riordan, M., Iwata, B., Finney, J., *et al* (1984) Behavioural assessment and treatment of chronic food refusal in handicapped children. *Journal of Applied Behaviour Analysis*, **17**, 327–341.

Roberts, L. (1996) Fat is a children's issue. *Nursery World*, **96**, 8–10.

Russell, G. (1970) Anorexia nervosa: its identity as an illness and its treatment. In *Modern Trends in Psychological Medicine* (ed. J. Price). London: Butterworth.

——, Szmukler, G., Dare, C., *et al* (1987) An evaluation of family therapy in anorexia nervosa and bulimia nervosa. *Archives of General Psychiatry*, **44**, 1047–1056.

Rutter, M., Tizzard, J. & Whitmore, K. (eds) (1981) *Education, Health, Behaviour*. New York: Kriger Huntington.

Rydell, A. M., Dahl, M. & Sundelin, C. (1995) Characteristics of school children who are choosy eaters. *Journal of Genetic Psychology*, **156**, 217–229.

Sanders, M. R., Patel, R. K., Le Grice, B., *et al* (1993) Children with persistent feeding difficulties: An observational analysis of the feeding interaction of problem and non-problem eaters. *Health Psychology*, **12**, 64–73.

Shaffer, D., Gould, M., Brasic, J., *et al* (1983) A Children's Global Assessment Scale (GAS). *Archives of General Psychiatry*, **40**, 1228–1231.

Sharpe, C. W. & Freeman, C. P. (1993) Medical complications of anorexia nervosa. *British Journal of Psychiatry*, **162**, 452.

Singer, L. T., Ambuel, B., Wade, S., *et al* (1992) Cognitive–behavioural treatment of health-impairing food phobias in children. *Journal of the American Academy of Child and Adolescent Psychiatry*, **31**, 847–852.

Skuse, D. (1985) Non-organic failure to thrive: a reappraisal. *Archives of Disease in Childhood*, **60**, 173–178.

Smolak, L. & Levine, M. P. (1994) Toward an empirical basis for primary prevention of eating problems with elementary school children. *Eating Disorders: The Journal of Treatment and Prevention*, **2**, 293–307.

Stein, A., Woolley, H. & McPherson, K. (1999) Conflict between mothers with eating disorders and their infants during mealtimes. *British Journal of Psychiatry*, **175**, 455–461.

Steinhausen, H-C. (1997) Annotation: Outcome of anorexia nervosa in the younger patient. *Journal of Child Psychology and Psychiatry*, **38**, 271–276.

Stice, E., Agras, W. S. & Hammer, L. D. (1999) Risk factors for the emergence of childhood eating disturbances: a five-year prospective study. *International Journal of Eating Disorders*, **25**, 375–387.

Swift, W. J. (1982) The long-term outcome of early onset anorexia nervosa: A critical review. *Journal of the American Academy of Child Psychiatry*, **21**, 38–46.

Timimi, S., Douglas, J. & Tsiftsopoulou, K. (1997) Selective eaters: a retrospective case note study. *Child Care Health and Development*, **23**, 256–278.

Turner, K. M. T., Sanders, M. R. & Wall, C. R. (1994) Behavioural parent training versus dietary education in the treatment of children with persistent feeding difficulties. *Behaviour Change*, **11**, 242–258.

Wada, S., Nagase, T., Koike, Y., *et al* (1992) A case of anorexia nervosa with acute renal failure induced by rhabdomyolysis: Possible involvement of hypophosphatemia or phosphate depletion. *Internal Medicine*, **31**, 478–482.

Waldholtz, B. D. & Andersen, A. E. (1990) Gastrointestinal symptoms in anorexia nervosa: A prospective study. *Gastroenterology*, **98**, 1415–1419.

Warady, B. A., Kriely. M., Belkden, B., *et al* (1990) Nutritional and behavioural aspects of nasogastric tube feeding in infants receiving chronic peritoneal dialysis. *Advances in Peritoneal Dialysis*, **6**, 265–268.

Warren, W. (1968) A study of anorexia nervosa in young girls. *Journal of Child Psychology and Psychiatry*, **9**, 27–40.

Werle, M. A., Murphy, T. B. & Budd, K. S. (1993) Treating chronic food refusal in young children: home-based parent training. *Journal of Applied and Behavioural Analysis*, **26**, 421–433.

Whitehouse, P. J. & Harris, G. (1998) The inter-generational transmission of eating disorders. *European Eating Disorders Review*, **6**, 238–254.

Whiting, M. & Lobstein, T. (1992) Children with eating problems. *In The Nursery Food Book*. London: Edward Arnold.

Wittenberg, J. P. (1990) Feeding disorders in infancy: Classification and treatment considerations. *Canadian Journal of Psychiatry*, **35**, 529–533.

World Health Organization (1992) *The ICD–10 Classification of Mental and Behavioural Disorders: Clinical Descriptions and Diagnostic Guidelines*. Geneva: WHO.

SELECTED INFORMATION SOURCES

Research in progress

National Research Register
The Cochrane Library
CRD Ongoing Reviews Database

Major databases

MEDLINE
Embase
Database of Abstracts of Reviews of Effectiveness (DARE)
Cochrane Database of Systematic Reviews (CDSR)
Psychological Abstracts (PsycLit)

SEARCH QUESTION

Population	Intervention	Outcome
Children with eating problems	Any	Any

Synonyms

Eating disorder
Eating difficulties
Feeding problems
Feeding disorder
Feeding difficulties

Different types of disorder

FAED
Pervasive refusal syndrome
Selective eating/extreme faddiness
Functional dysphagia/food phobia

Food refusal
Restrictive eating/poor appetite
Inappropriate texture of food for age
Refusal to sit down
Organic/non-organic failure to thrive

SEARCH STRATEGIES

MEDLINE 1

No.	Records	Request
1	219419	child*
2	43210	food
3	5770	avoidance
4	7739	emotional
5	47647	disorder
6	0	child* and food avoidance emotional disorder
7	219419	child*
8	3346	anorexia
9	1940	nervosa
10	8	child* anorexia nervosa
11	43402	young
12	219419	child*
13	3346	anorexia
14	1940	nervosa
15	3	young child* anorexia nervosa
16	118013	infant*
17	10933	eating
18	153958	prob*
19	5	infant* and eating prob*
20	118013	infant*
21	10933	eating
22	147467	disorder*
23	12	infant* and eating disorder*
24	368733	treatment*
25	118013	infant*
26	10933	eating
27	147467	disorder*
28	21	treatment* and infant* and eating disorder*
29	27768	pediatric
30	18420	feeding
31	147467	disorder*
32	6	pediatric feeding disorder*
33	219419	child*
34	43402	young
35	2538	dysphagia
36	2	young child* and dysphagia

PSYCLIT 1

No.	Records	Request
1	44920	child*
2	4163	food
3	3555	avoidance
4	14792	emotional
5	31220	disorder
6	1	child* and food avoidance emotional disorder
7	44920	child*
8	2250	anorexia
9	2827	nervosa
10	359	child* and anorexia nervosa
11	8263	young
12	44920	child*
13	2250	anorexia
14	2827	nervosa
15	26	young and child* and anorexia nervosa
16	8263	young
17	44920	child*
18	2250	anorexia
19	2827	nervosa
20	1	young child* and anorexia nervosa
21	44920	child*
22	4434	eating
23	21933	problems
24	25	child* and eating problems
25	8263	young
26	44920	child*
27	4434	eating
28	69607	disorder
29	10	young child* and eating disorder
30	5964	infant*
31	4434	eating
32	35693	prob*
33	7	infant* and eating prob*
34	62079	treatment*
35	8263	young
36	44920	child*
37	4434	eating
38	21933	problems
39	1	treatment* and young child* and eating problems
40	62079	treatment*
41	44920	child*
42	4434	eating
43	29775	problem*
44	10	treatment* and child* and eating problem*
45	62079	treatment*

46	8263	young
47	44920	child*
48	2250	anorexia
49	2827	nervosa
50	0	treatment* and young child* and anorexia nervosa
51	62079	treatment*
52	8263	young
53	44920	child*
54	4434	eating
55	69607	disorder*
56	4	treatment* and young child* and eating disorder*

EMBASE 2

No.	Records	Request
1	46800	selective
2	18437	eat*
3	231008	child*
4	6	(selective near5 eat*) and child*
5	2195	restrictive
6	17	(restrictive near5 #2) and #3
7	27939	food
8	6823	phobia
9	0	(food near5 phobia) and #3
10	211	fuss*
11	6	(fuss* near10 #2) and #3
12	4733	refus*
13	118	(#7 near10 #12) and #3

MEDLINE 2

Systematic review and meta-analysis search strategy as provided by The NHS CRD.

critical appraisal tools

LONGITUDINAL SURVEYS OR CASE SERIES

Citation . . . .

Is the study based on a random sample selected from a suitable sampling frame?	Yes ❏	No ❏	Cannot tell ❏
Is there any evidence that the sample is representative of standard users of the intervention?	Yes ❏	No ❏	Cannot tell ❏
Are the criteria for inclusion in the sample clearly defined?	Yes ❏	No ❏	Cannot tell ❏
Did all individuals enter the survey at a similar point in their disease progression?	Yes ❏	No ❏	Cannot tell ❏
Was follow-up long enough for important events to occur?	Yes ❏	No ❏	Cannot tell ❏
Were outcomes assessed using objective criteria?	Yes ❏	No ❏	Cannot tell ❏
If comparisons of series are being made, was there sufficient description of the series and the distribution of prognostic factors?	Yes ❏	No ❏	Cannot tell ❏

CROSS-SECTIONAL OR FOLLOW-UP STUDY (COHORT STUDIES)

Citation . . . .

How was the study population selected?

Do the subjects come from a hospital in-patient or out-patient group, from a general practice or from the community? Were there particular features or characteristics of the subjects that influenced their selection? Have they already been through a selective filter in the medical system? Will the study population be comparable with other groups?

Comments:

Have the procedures for sampling within this population been defined (eligibility criteria)?

Yes ❏   No ❏   Cannot tell ❏

Is it clear how individual subjects were selected and in what manner to avoid selection bias?

Yes ❏   No ❏   Cannot tell ❏

Do the authors include exclusion criteria?

Yes ❏   No ❏   Cannot tell ❏

Is the potential for selection bias recognised? Have steps been taken to avoid it or is there evidence that the problem has not affected the results?

Yes ❏   No ❏   Cannot tell ❏

If a cross-sectional study, have antecedent–consequent relationships been made clear?

Yes ❏   No ❏   Cannot tell ❏

If subjects have been classified by potentially causative characteristics as well as effects and outcomes, has a cause and effect relationship been implied?

Yes ❏   No ❏   Cannot tell ❏

Is it possible that the characteristic leads to the outcome or is it likely that certain diseases secondarily acquire characteristics that appear causal?

Comments:

If a follow-up design, is there any loss to follow-up?

Yes ❏   No ❏   Cannot tell ❏

Have the authors described in detail the method of following up subjects and given information about those remained?

Yes ❏   No ❏   Cannot tell ❏

Has drop out led to biased results?

Yes ❏   No ❏   Cannot tell ❏

Is it likely that the attrition rate is related to outcomes under study such as side-effects?

Yes ❏   No ❏   Cannot tell ❏

Did the therapy, lifestyle or behaviour of any subjects change during the study?

Yes ❏   No ❏   Cannot tell ❏

Has observation bias occurred? ie: did both groups receive comparable observation?

Yes ❏   No ❏   Cannot tell ❏

OBSERVATIONAL – CASE CONTROL STUDY

Citation . . . .

Is information from the past dependable?	Yes ❑	No ❑	Cannot tell ❑
Are data available from well-documented medical records with data recorded in a reliable method?	Yes ❑	No ❑	Cannot tell ❑

Comments:

If data have been recorded based on the recollection of subjects, is recall bias operating?	Yes ❑	No ❑	Cannot tell ❑
What attempts have the authors made to assess the effect of this potential bias?	Yes ❑	No ❑	Cannot tell ❑
How alike are the control group? Are they really from a similar population differing only in the absence of disease?	Yes ❑	No ❑	Cannot tell ❑

Comments:

Are there any other differences that might bear a relation on the outcome being studied and might give a spurious appearance of relationship between the attribute being studied and the outcome?	Yes ❑	No ❑	Cannot tell ❑

Comments:

Have matching techniques been used in an attempt to control such confounding relationships?	Yes ❑	No ❑	Cannot tell ❑
What kind of population do the cases represent? Are they a heterogeneous representation of the disease or outcome being studied or a highly selected population for whom the responses may have limited generalisability?	Yes ❑	No ❑	Cannot tell ❑

Are other biases evident? Is more known about the cases because they have received closer surveillance, volunteered more information or been subjected to more tests than the control group?

Comments:

assessment of study quality

CASE SERIES

Point allocation

	Answer:		
Question	Yes	No	Cannot tell
Is the study based on a random sample selected from a suitable sampling frame?	2	0	1
Is there any evidence that the sample is representative of standard users of the intervention?	2	0	1
Are the criteria for inclusion in the sample clearly defined?	2	0	1
Did all individuals enter the survey at a similar point in their disease progression?	2	0	1
Was follow-up long enough for important events to occur?	2	0	1
Were outcomes assessed using objective criteria?	2	0	1
If comparisons of series are being made, was there sufficient description of the series and the distribution of prognostic factors?	2	0	1

COHORT STUDIES

Point allocation

Question	Answer:		
	Yes	No	Cannot tell
Have the procedures for sampling within this population been defined (eligibility criteria)?	2	0	1
Is it clear how individual subjects were selected and in what manner to avoid selection bias?	2	0	1
Do the authors include exclusion criteria?	2	0	1
Is the potential for selection bias recognised? Have steps been taken to avoid it or is there evidence that the problem has not affected the results?	2	0	1
If a follow-up design, is there any loss to follow-up?	0	2	1
Have the authors described in detail the method of following up subjects and given information about those remained?	2	0	1
Has drop-out led to biased results?	0	2	1
Is it likely that the attrition rate is related to outcomes under study such as side-effects?	0	2	1
Did the therapy, lifestyle or behaviour of any subjects change during the study?	0	2	1
Has observation bias occurred? ie: did both groups receive comparable observation?	2	0	1

CASE-CONTROL STUDIES

Point allocation

Question	Answer: Yes	No	Cannot tell
Is information from the past dependable?	2	0	1
Are data available from well-documented medical records with data recorded in a reliable method?	2	0	1
If data have been recorded based on the recollection of subjects, is recall bias operating?	0	2	1
What attempts have the authors made to assess the effect of this potential bias?	2	0	1
How alike are the control group? Are they really from a similar population differing only in the absence of disease?	2	0	1
Are there any other differences that might bear a relation on the outcome being studied and might give a spurious appearance of relationship between the attribute being studied and the outcome?	0	2	1
Have matching techniques been used in an attempt to control such confounding relationships?	2	0	1
What kind of population do the cases represent? Are they a heterogenous representation of the disease or outcome being studied or a highly selected population for whom the responses may have limited generalisability?	2 (Representative)	0 (Highly selected)	1
Are other biases evident? Is more known about the cases because they have received closer surveillance, volunteered more information or been subjected to more tests than the control group?	0	2	1

appendix iv assessment of a child's growth potential

ADULT HEIGHT POTENTIAL

The adult height, which a child should expect to achieve genetically if his or her growth is absolutely normal, is called the mid-parental height (MPH). This is usually referred to in terms of one of the printed centiles on the centile chart – the mid-parental centile (MPC). Children may not always follow their mid-parental centile exactly, but all should grow within specific centiles, called their target centile range (TCR).

Calculation of a boy's mid-parental height/mid-parental centile

In order to calculate the MPH/MPC of a boy, it is important to know the height of both parents of the child. To give an example, the MPH/MPC of a boy whose father is 176 cm tall and whose mother is 160 cm tall would be calculated as follows:

(a)   First, add the height (in centimetres) of the father to the height (in centimetres) of the mother: 176 cm + 160 cm = 336 cm.
(b)   Divide your answer by 2:   336 cm/2 = 168 cm.
(c)   Add 7 cm to your answer: 168 cm + 7 cm = 175 cm.
(d)   175 cm is his MPH – this can now be marked on a growth chart to the right of the 18-year line found on the horizontal axis (see Fig. 1).
(e)   His MPC is the printed centile found on the growth chart nearest to his MPH – in this example this would be the 50th centile.
(f)   His TCR is bordered by the two centiles 10 cm above and 10 cm below his MPH – that is, between the centiles found on the growth chart at 185 cm and 165 cm. In this case, therefore, his TCR is between the 91st centile and the 9th centile. This means that he should be growing within these two centiles from the age of 2 years.

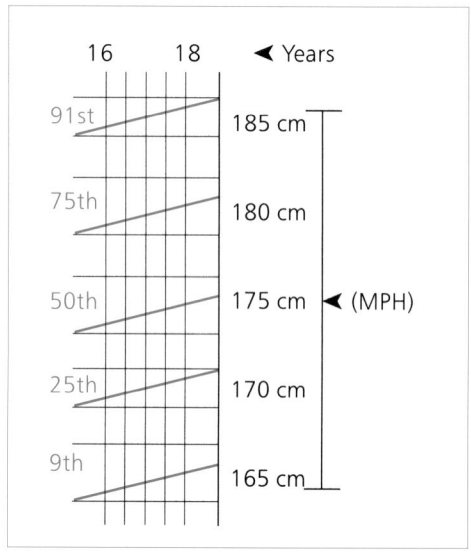

Fig. 1 Diagram to illustrate part of a growth chart for a boy (blue diagonal lines are centiles)

Calculation of a girl's mid-parental height/mid-parental centile

In order to calculate the MPH/MPC of a girl, it is important to know the height of both parents of the child. To give an example, the MPH/MPC of a girl whose father is 186 cm tall and whose mother is 156 cm tall would be calculated as follows:

(a) First, add the height (in centimetres) of the father to the height (in centimetres) of the mother: 186 cm + 156 cm = 342 cm.

(b) Divide your answer by 2:   342 cm/2 = 171 cm.

(c) Subtract 7 cm from your answer: 171 cm – 7 cm = 164 cm.

(d) 164 cm is her MPH – this can now be marked on a growth chart to the right of the 18-year line found on the horizontal axis (see Fig. 2).

(e) Her MPC is the printed centile found on the growth chart nearest to her MPH – in this example this would be the 50th centile.

(f) Her TCR is bordered by the two centiles 8.5 cm above and 8.5 cm below her MPH – that is, between the centiles found on the growth chart at 172.5 cm and 155.5 cm. In this case, therefore, her TCR is between the 91st centile and the 9th centile. This means that she should be growing within these two centiles from the age of 2 years.

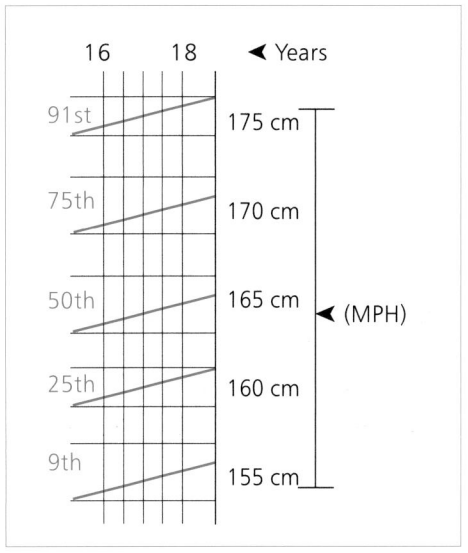

Fig. 2 Diagram to illustrate part of a growth chart for a girl (blue diagonal lines are centiles)

The addition or subtraction of 7 cm is to compensate for the average difference between the heights of Caucasian (White) men and women.

For further details, contact The Child Growth Foundation (see Useful addresses, p. 62).

index